Walking

With

Tigers

Walking
With
Tigers

One Refugee's Amazing
Story of Survival

The Story of Shoua Her

by

Lynann Butler, Ph.D.

Storytellers Publishing

Colorado, USA

Storytellers Publishing
An imprint of Journey Institute Press,
a division of 50 in 52 Journey, Inc.
journeyinstitutepress.org

Library of Congress Control Number: In Process
Names: Butler, Lynann
Title: WALKING WITH TIGERS
Description: Colorado: Storytellers Publishing, 2024

Identifiers: ISBN 978-1-964754-12-3 (paperback)
978-1-964754-13-0 (ebook/kindle)
Subjects: BISAC:
BIOGRAPHY & AUTOBIOGRAPHY / Asian & Asian American
BIOGRAPHY & AUTOBIOGRAPHY / Cultural & Regional
BIOGRAPHY & AUTOBIOGRAPHY / Survival

Second Edition
Printed in the United States of America
2 4 7 10 15 30 34 40 61 86

This book was typeset in Baskerville URW / Footlight MT Light

Cover Photo by the Author
Cover Design by WiggleB Studios

Photo Credits:
All photos taken by the Author unless otherwise indicated.

Contents

Foreword

He couldn't remember not being hungry. With an empty belly and tired feet, the boy trudged through the leaves and vines of the jungle floor, picking his way through the minefield to catch up with his mother. As he made his way to one of the outlying bamboo shelters, Shoua heard a noise he hadn't discerned before- a tearing, crunching sound. He rounded the bamboo cluster and was startled to see a tiger on the trail directly in front of him. The beast had a thick reddish striped coat and a white belly and was ripping into the flesh of a corpse. The tiger turned, its enormous paws now at a 90-degree angle to the child. The boy held his breath, unable to move. Fear rooted him to the spot even as a part of his brain screamed for him to run. The tiger spotted him and hesitated, sniffing the air. Its eyes seemed to look right through Shoua and the boy felt the air escape his lungs. His nerves taut and muscles tense, Shoua stood frozen in place and felt as if the world had shifted into slow motion. The tiger licked its mouth, its white and black tail twitching from side to side before slowly turning towards the trees. The giant cat lumbered into the forest, leaving behind its meal/victim. Shoua crumpled to the ground, unable to move for several moments. The rush of adrenaline that had attacked his body made him feel physically sick and he fought back a wave of nausea as he sat on the jungle floor. He focused on his breathing, willing it to return to normal so he could make his way back to his mother. The only safe way back to his family- the route that was known to be free of landmines- was the path the child and the tiger had shared. He tried to catch his breath- what if the tiger came back? What if it wasn't hunting alone?

Introduction

You could hear a pin drop. The class sits silently, listening with rapt attention. No one takes notes or utters a whisper, such is the effect Shoua Her has on my Multicultural Issues class when he comes to guest lecture and share his story. Several years ago, the gentleman who usually volunteered to guest speak during our Asian American unit informed me that he had a conflict in his schedule and wouldn't be able to present in my class. Panicked, I called the local Asian Pacific Development Center asking for a speaker knowledgeable about such issues and willing to share his or her story. Enter Shoua. I have had the great honor of listening to Shoua's jaw-dropping tales of survival every semester for years now as he generously returns to each new class I teach. The students sit riveted as he describes his story, complete with landmines, tigers, starvation, enormous personal loss and hardship. After a half dozen times of telling him, "Your story is so amazing... Someone should write a book about you!" I finally did just that. After many hours of interviews and endless research, this book is about Shoua and the tens of thousands of Hmong people who surmounted incredible odds as they escaped persecution in Laos. All historic details are relayed with as much accuracy as possible.

Chapter 1
The Hmong and the Secret War in Laos

President Eisenhower sat at a large oval table with his hands clasped lightly on the wooden surface. He listened as his advisors requested aid to France, which was struggling to keep its colonial rule in Vietnam (Ho Chi Minh had declared Vietnam to be an independent Democratic Republic of Vietnam). The advisors explained their concerns about the "falling domino" theory, the seemingly inevitable spread of communism throughout Southeast Asia if the small country of Laos were to fall under communist rule. The interest in Laos centered on the Ho Chi Minh Trail, which ran through the country and was used as a significant artery to move troops, weapons, medicine and other supplies from North to South Vietnam. North Vietnam, the former French colony, wanted Vietnam united as one communist country. South Vietnam was interested in remaining separate and in maintaining a more western government structure. If the North Vietnamese had unencumbered access to the Ho Chi Minh Trail, their efforts at subjugating South Vietnam would be that much easier. The trail served a critical function in the communist takeover and by the end of the war would be used by two million people and to move forty-five million tons of cargo.

Figure 1, Map of Laos [Photo Credit: jasejla
Under license by: Envato Elements, License Code:WTKDPNYJQ5

Eisenhower nodded his head slowly as he realized what his advisors were asking him to do. Sending sons into battle is never an easy task. Sending them across the world to a conflict that is not their own is even harder. But, his advisors reasoned, if the US did nothing, it would allow communism to spread unchecked. If Laos could be saved from communist takeover they would also have saved Cambodia, South Vietnam, Thailand and Burma. By containing the communist threat, Eisenhower and his advisors believed they could save the much larger region. "What about the Geneva Conference?" an advisor pointed out, citing the 1954 meeting that addressed issues in Korea, peace in Indochina (Vietnam, Cambodia, and Laos) and significantly, established Laos as a neutral country. (Note: This differs from the 1949 Geneva Convention, which addressed victims of war, including civilians and prisoners of war.) "As much as we'd like to keep the communists out of Laos, we can't march in there with troops!"

A White House aide brought the President some refreshment. He savored the prune whip, his favorite dessert, and listened to the discussion around him. Someone suggested getting Thai fighters involved, but that too would have been a violation of the Geneva Conference. It was finally settled that the US would assist Laos and help to keep it from becoming the first domino to fall to communism without engaging American forces. The United States would continue to send in airmen to drop supplies to French forces already engaged in Indochina and would expand the service to include the conflict in Laos. The US would also help to train the existing Royal Lao Army. In this way, the people of Laos could fight their own battle with funding and support offered very quietly by the United States. It would be another ten years before the United States would engage in outright armed combat in Laos.

As the discussion wound down, President Eisenhower retired to the Blue Room where he enjoyed painting in order to relax. He arranged his easel and brushes and lined up the paints he would use, feeling the knots in his neck already begin to loosen as he began his hobby. He chose colors from the palate to fill in the lines already on the canvas before him. Because Eisenhower did not have the skills to sketch, someone else had to provide the lines in which he would paint, thus allowing him the satisfaction of creating art while bypassing the challenge of his inability to draw. This eventually triggered the paint-by-numbers hobby around the country. As he concentrated on his brushstrokes, the President reflected on the day's briefing. He was pleased with the progress of the meeting and the decisions that were made. He had no way of knowing that the continued threat of communism would later engage Presidents Kennedy, Johnson, and Nixon.

As a result of the decisions to quietly assist in Laos, American troops had been operating in that country since 1957 without the awareness of American citizens. In fact, even John F. Kennedy was not aware of the US presence in Laos until Eisenhower informed him the day before Kennedy's presidential inauguration. The CIA was able to keep the mission a secret from the media and the public by employing very creative strategies. According to Keith Quincy in *Harvesting Pa Chay's Wheat*, it was:

> …as if the American aircraft did not exist. In a sense, they didn't. Many had been laundered by the CIA, with duplicates bearing the same markings and engine numbers showing up at various airfields across the globe to be duly logged in while their twins were over Laos on combat

missions. If the planes were shot down, the CIA possessed documentation proving they were still flying and nowhere near Laos. Some Air Force planes were completely sanitized after delivery to the CIA, with all military insignia and engine numbers removed, essentially having no documented existence. Other planes were removed from USAF records by being sold as military surplus to the pilots who flew them. The buyers, identified in the bills of sale as civilian aviators, were all US Air Force personnel dropped from the military rolls and listed as forest rangers with the United States Agency for International Development (USAID). The planes carried a price tag of a dollar each.

The covert assistance in Laos continued under President Kennedy, who condoned the use of "The Third Option", or continued support of forces native to the area. The US supported General Vang Pao, the Hmong military leader who commanded local guerilla fighters in the area by sending Air America supply drops, funding of local troops and training in counterinsurgency techniques. Many of the fighters used in The Third Option were the Hmong people from the mountains of northern Laos. The reasons for engaging the Hmong were many. They knew the mountains better than anyone and were brilliant guerrilla warriors. The Hmong were excellent at fight and melt-back-into-the-jungle tactics. Additionally, they were brave and fierce and able to run up the side of a mountain as few of the American soldiers had ever witnessed. The Hmong were imbued with a sense of motivation that no foreign soldier could comprehend, as it was their homeland they were defending.

The Hmong fought the communists in coordination with the Central Intelligence Agency. Many of the Hmong involved in the war went unpaid while 30,000 Hmong were paid 10 cents a day per person, or $2 to $3 a month. They served a number of roles in the collaborative effort. Most were warriors using the grenades and M16 rifles provided by the US military. Some men flew as spotters operating behind the cockpit of reconnaissance planes where they could identify locations effectively as they knew every tree line and river boundary in the area. Flying reconnaissance missions was dangerous.

A United States Army pilot who flew Forward Air Control during the Vietnam War shared his experiences. Don Nelson was flying an L19, called a Birddog, a two-seater front-to-back plane made by Cessna. The Birddogs were used for visual and photo reconnaissance and search and rescue missions during the wars in Southeast Asia. Nelson flew with 2.75 rockets, four under each wing. Usually he carried half explosives (for defense), half with white phosphorous smoke used to mark targets for future bombing runs. His job was to fly low and search for the Vietcong, which he did by peering through the jungle foliage for signs of the enemy. He would look for any changes to the environment, including bridges across streams, fresh trails and anti-aircraft positions. Sometimes he could spot camouflaged bunkers or fox-holes that had been recently dug. He recalled that the VC were very difficult to spot as they used camouflage cleverly, squatting low and tying bushes and branches onto their backs. The only time they could be seen was when they moved.

One day, Chief Warrant Officer Nelson was training a new Army recruit pilot. He explained to the recruit that they would only get one chance to spot the enemy. He was usually able to fly over them once and the VC would not shoot. Make a second pass, however, and it was another story. (If the Vietcong fired at the plane they gave away their position and soon became artillery targets. Occasionally a new VC would make that mistake and would be hit later by air strikes.) As the Birddog flew low over the jungle trees, Nelson saw evidence of the enemy. He spoke through the headset, alerting the new pilot in the front seat what he saw and what to look for. It is very challenging to spot camouflaged troops in the jungle if you don't know what to look for, and the new recruit missed the signs. The trainee requested a second recon pass to get another look. Nelson grudgingly acquiesced. They flew in low again, as flying high exposed the plane to enemy fire too easily. Because it was their second pass, the VC knew they had been spotted and opened fire. Nelson and the new pilot heard the pop-pop-pop sound as bullets screamed around them from the automatic weapons being fired from the jungle floor. The bullets broke the sound barrier as they tore through the air. Nelson, flying just above the trees, pushed the nose of the aircraft down to avoid enemy fire, creating a negative G force. If a person is sitting static and weighs 110 pounds, they are at 1 G, or one force of gravity. If they go into two positive G's it is as if the person weighs 220 pounds and they are pushed *into* the seat. The two pilots of the Birddog found themselves in negative G force, held in only by the seat belt straps in the aircraft. Because of the negative G forces the stick came out of the floor- Nelson was left holding a stick and did not have control of the plane! He spoke through the headset to the new pilot who was sitting in the front of the plane, "Pull up! Pull up!" until he realized the wires in the headset (that connect through the stick) were no longer connected either. He began screaming the order instead. As the plane began plummeting towards the jungle floor, the new pilot somehow heard the order and was able to pull them out of a crash at the last second.

Figure 2, Photo Credit: manhhai https://www.flickr.com/photos/13476480@N07/10448037636/
1967 Cessna 0-1E Bird Dog aircraft
A U.S. Air Force Cessna 0-1E Bird Dog aircraft (serialn number 56-4200) in flight over Vietnam in 1967
Licensed under CC Attribution 4.0 International
https://creativecommons.org/licenses/by/4.0/

The Birddog planes flown by Nelson and other brave US pilots are the ones identified by the subject of this book as aircraft abandoned by the US military when they pulled out of Laos in 1975. The planes were confiscated by the Vietminh who used them against the Hmong.

Hmong men served as pilots, usually in a T-28, a US military training plane. Because of their small stature, the men would have to place pillows on their seats and blocks of wood under their feet to reach the foot controls of the planes.

Figure 3, Photo Credit: LoadedAaron https://www.flickr.com/ photos/92854517@N00/37061585096/
T-28
Licensed under CC Attribution 4.0 International
https://creativecommons.org/licenses/by/4.0/

One of the best known Hmong T-28 pilots was Major Lue Ly (Lee is the westernized version of Ly). According to Keith Quincy, Ly "was in the air nearly every day, sometimes flying nonstop for up to ten hours, his arms and legs so cramped a flight crew had to pry him out of the plane…. Lue Ly's trademark, however, was his low approach, skimming the ground until he released his ordinance, almost hand-delivering bombs to the enemy. Sometimes when he returned his propeller was covered with the blood of NVA who had failed to duck when he made his pass." Lue Ly flew over five thousand sorties overall before he was shot down and killed. His motto, "Fly 'til you die" was the battle cry explaining that being a Hmong pilot was for all intents and purposes a death sentence. Hmong pilots knew the job would eventually kill them, as there was no retirement from this responsibility during the war. While American pilots received R&R (Rest & Relaxation) time and eventually were sent home after completing their missions, the Hmong pilots continued to fly until they were killed or captured.

A close cousin of the subject of this book was training to become a pilot of the T-28. The cousin, whose name was Tong Ying Her, was learning to fly. He was in the front seat of the plane, the instructor in the back. They took off from the base in Udon, Thailand, the site of a major US Air Force base during the war. Tong Ying soon encountered severe technical difficulties with the plane. When it became clear that they would not be able to safely land, Tong Ying told the instructor to bail out and then he would bail next (Hmong T-28s had no ejection seats at all until 1968 so pilots flew at even greater risk before that time). The instructor ejected and landed safely. Perhaps due to foggy weather conditions, when Tong Ying was flying low to the ground he had inverted the plane without realizing it, so when he tried to open his chute, the force drove him into the ground instead of up into the air. He was one of many deaths of Hmong pilots during that era.

Other Hmong served as search and rescue.

Shouts called over the radio- an American fighter plane had been hit! The two airmen were fortunate enough to have ejected before impact and landed in a dry rice paddy. Forty Hmong men and boys were dispatched to retrieve them. It was estimated they had approximately fifteen minutes in which to locate and rescue the crew before it was considered a lost cause. If the airmen were not rescued in that timeframe, chances were good the Viet Minh had captured them and the lost airmen faced a daunting future of torture and starvation. Not all of the Hmong rescuers survived these forays into the war zone. They risked their lives- dozens of Hmong men for two Americans–without fanfare, hazard pay or glory. On some missions, as many as 100 Hmong ran to the downed plane as part of the rescue effort and only 40 survived. Sometimes the communists had already captured the American pilots and were lying in wait at the site of the crash to kill any Hmong who arrived as part of the rescue effort. These Hmong men and boys remain a minor footnote in history.

The fighting had gone on for over 20 years and as a result the number of adult men able to fight in the war was dwindling. Over one third of the male Hmong population had been killed, including half of all males over the age of fifteen. As a result, 70% of new warrior recruits consisted of boys aged ten to sixteen. According to an account cited in Her & Buley-Meissner's book, *Hmong and American; from Refugees to Citizens,* "By 1970, twelve- and thirteen-year-old Hmong boys were replacing their fathers, uncles and older brothers killed in battle: 'The boys were no taller than their rifles. They disappeared inside their uniforms, and walked out of their boots when they marched'. These boys were often referred to as "carbine soldiers" since they were barely taller than the carbine rifles they carried. While the Hmong don't traditionally have a period of adolescence–kids go from children to adulthood through early marriage and parenthood–these boys had to grow up fast even by Hmong standards. They quickly learned to become soldiers. To become men.

The far-reaching consequences to the Hmong and other indigenous people of Laos could not have been foreseen. During the war, the North Vietnamese grabbed whatever lands they could in Laos, displacing tens of thousands of people. There was no safe place to rest, no "shore leave", no GI benefits, no well-deserved time off. It was fight or die. The death toll for the Hmong was staggering. It has been reported that between 30,000 and 40,000 Hmong died during the Secret War in Laos.

As the war raged on and so many young American men were being killed in Southeast Asia with no discernable progress being made, the anti-war sentiment in America grew stronger. The United States government began to explore an exit strategy from the region. In the early 1970s the decision was made by the Nixon Administration to pull American troops out of Vietnam and Laos. It was when the last of the Americans pulled out of the region in 1975 and left the Hmong to fight for themselves that the real troubles began. This was a confusing time for the Hmong, as they had been promised that America would take care of them in payment for their contribution to the war effort. The critical US air support that had covered Hmong ground fighting had been significantly reduced and eventually eliminated, leaving them vulnerable to the guns of the Pathet Lao troops. Many Hmong were forced to flee or face being hunted down, captured or killed.

The Royal Lao government collapsed in 1975 and a new communist government emerged called the Lao People's Democratic Republic, or the Pathet Lao (North Vietnam's version of the Viet Minh). Both the Pathet Lao and the Viet Minh were intent on destroying the Hmong. The Hmong had become targets of extermination due to their assistance to the Americans during the war and their reticence in assimilating into communist rule. Any remaining Hmong who had not already been killed or evacuated were in danger and actively sought after by communist troops. Hmong warriors who had battled alongside the Americans against the North Vietnamese or the Pathet Lao were hunted down and killed or taken to "seminar camps", a sugary term for concentration camps. The Royal Family of Laos was imprisoned in a seminar camp where, deprived of fresh air and natural light, they all eventually starved to death. (The Royal Palace where the family had lived in the former capital of Luang Prabang is now a museum.) Prisoners in the camps were subjected to torture, hard labor, and daily anti-American/pro-communist propaganda. Prisoners were forced to dig holes and trenches all day in the hot sun for no purpose, and lived on starvation level rations–in some cases as little as 500 grams of rice and 20 grams of salt per month. They were given no shoes, no medical attention, and allowed very little sleep. In some camps, 25 men were housed in a 7 by 15 meter hut. Some were chained at night, others put into holes where they starved to death.

Some families chose to remain in their mountain home-land, deciding it was better under their circumstances to try to live under communist rule than to relocate. They buried their weapons and destroyed their uniforms and any evidence of their participation in the war against the Vietnamese and the Pathet Lao. All it took was for one person to recognize a former soldier, however, or to misspeak about the past and the family's life may be on the line. Soldiers from North Vietnam would come to villages to interview each member of a family that remained in order to determine the loyalties of that family. If it was decided during the course of that interview that a family member needed to "learn a new system", the head of the household was taken away. Family members never saw them again, as most were taken to the seminar camps.

Some of the Hmong soldiers who were forced to flee were airlifted to the safety of Thailand, but there were simply not enough aircraft or American personnel still in Laos to evac-uate the remaining families. It was complete mayhem as the last of the rescue helicopters were leaving Laos in 1975. Over forty thousand desperate people crowded to the airfield where craft were available for only fifteen thousand refugees. Family members pushed to get aboard, overcrowding the planes and helicopters sent to carry them to safety before the final push of the communists destroyed whoever remained.

> So many people clambered to get aboard the cargo planes that often the crews could not close the ramps for takeoff. To get people away from the plane, the crews dumped duffle bags full of Lao kip [currency] onto the tarmac. As Hmong scurried to gather up the kip, the crew closed the ramp and the pilots gunned the engines. Propeller wash sent the kip aloft. Realizing what had just happened, the abandoned Hmong wept amid a confetti of money (Her & Buley-Meissner, p. 69).

Figure 4, This was the type of plane that carried Shoua and his family from Long Tieng to Na Su. The cargo opened waist-high - Shoua was so little his dad had to lift him up and throw him inside. Photo courtesy of Shoua Her (used with permission)

Over a hundred thousand Hmong would soon be seeking escape.

Perspective is interesting. Western texts portray the French colonialists as stubborn but beneficent colonialists who overtaxed the people of Laos. The Lao version reads, "Under the French colonialist yoke, the Lao people suffer severe poverty and hardship" and are "subject to barbarous slavery". The US version of events records the "defeat" at DienBiemPhu while the communists record the "victory" of that "liberated" area. In the west, Kaysone's leadership is described as a "regime" that "cruelly played with the American government" while the Democratic People's Republic of Laos, a communist government, refers to him as "Comrade Kaysone" and celebrates his victories over the "US Imperialists and their puppets". The National Museum in the capital of Laos proudly displays a well-used metal pot with a placard that explains, "Comrade Kayson Phomvihane's kettle used during the fighting against the US Imperialists." There are other displays showing his bag, binoculars, gun, riding whip, and canteen, all with similar placards. Regardless of which government is explaining the conflict, the Hmong did not fare well at the outcome of the war. It is estimated that one third of their population was decimated during the war and another third annihilated in the aftermath by the Pathet Lao and Viet Minh who continued their attempts at complete genocide for decades after the war had officially ended.

The Hmong are of a unique ethnic identity originally from China. Other ethnic communities (such as some Khmu groups) migrated from southeastern China due to conflicts there. The Hmong are one of the more recent arrivals to Laos, having fled during the late 1700s through the mid-1800s. During that time period, the Chinese government, in an effort to unite the country and create one Chinese identity, tried to force them to become "more Chinese". In doing so, they were thwarting–sometimes violently–smaller ethnic identities. It was under these circumstances that many Hmong fled to Laos, a southeastern Asian country that shares borders with Vietnam, Thailand, Cambodia, Myanmar (formerly Burma) and China. The Hmong settled in the mountains near the border of North Vietnam. While they resided in the country of Laos, they did not consider themselves Laotian and in fact the Laotians were not welcoming of Hmong people. They used to be called "Miao" (or "Meo", the name the French used for the Hmong), but advocated to be recognized as "Hmong" due to the negative connotation derived from the former nomenclature. While the word "slave" is not a direct derivation of the word in Chinese, "Miao" was used by the Chinese in a condescending way that implied both inferiority and subjugation.

Subjugation was something the Hmong loathed and fought against for centuries. Keith Quincy's *Harvesting Pa Chay's Wheat* recounts the words of a German anthropologist in the 1930s who was quoted as saying, "Their urge for independence, their fearlessness bordering on defiance of death, their glowing love for freedom, which had been strengthened through thousands of years of fighting against powerful oppressors and has given them the reputation of feared warriors, will perhaps make difficulties for the colonizer" (the French, at that time). This fearlessness and love of freedom has been seen over time as different groups tried to force governance, assimilation or extermination upon the Hmong.

The Hmong lived in bamboo thatched–roof shelters in villages in the high mountains of northern Laos until their lives and identities were once again disrupted. This time the threat was communism and the events of the 1960's through the 1980s would forever change the number of Hmong that survived, where they would live, and how they would begin to identify themselves as they fought for survival. These mountain dwellers lived, a people unto themselves, an ethnic group without country or borders. They lived and loved and died amongst their own clans and did not mingle with outsiders. In many ways, they were a people without a nation which is fitting, as 'Hmong' means 'free people' in the language of Hmong.

It would be many years before the Hmong felt free again.

Chapter 2
The Early Years

The branches of the banana trees waved wildly as the helicopter approached for decent. Dust grew thick as the Huey bumped onto the small clearing that had been hacked out of the thick vegetation. The men quickly removed the contents in the hold. Sometimes the cargo consisted of medical supplies, salt or rice for the villagers. Today it contained body bags enveloping the Hmong warriors who had fallen during the secret war in Laos. No one in the village needed to shout for the child to come quickly, since he could hear the blades whirring through the thick, humid air. The chopper meant a ride for the boy to go visit his older brother. Once the body bags were dragged out of the hold, he jumped on board and hung on for the ear thrumming flight to Long Tieng air base. The smell of the dead lingered in his nostrils as he glimpsed at the treetops and winding river below.

The boy was Shoua (pronounced Show-ah) and he was going to visit his older brother Vang at his post. Vang worked air control, loading and directing cargo planes and helicopters for the CIA during the Secret War in Laos. The transports would take supplies to the front lines, pick up refugees and haul away the dead. As the Americans began pulling out of Laos, anti-communist/pro-American fighters such as Vang–along with their families–became targets for capture and execution by the Pathet Lao.

Figure 1, This is one of the types of helicopters that dropped off supplies to the Hmong. Shoua rode in this type of craft when he would visit his brother Vang. Photo taken by author.

Figure 2, Shoua (on left) with his brother, Vang
Photo courtesy of Shoua Her (used with permission)

Figure 12, The airfield in Long Tieng where Vang worked. CIA Headquarters is on the left. Shoua Her (used with permission)

Shoua Her is a Hmong refugee who was born in Laos and emigrated to the United States in the 1970s. His first name means "Chinese" and his last name, Her, indicates his clan ("Her" is spelled "Hawj" in the Hmong language). In his culture, he would be known by his clan name first then his given name, but refugees have adapted to the American nomenclature. The Hers are one of eighteen clans in Hmong culture with other clan names that include Vang, Chue, Lee and Moua. His family, like so many Hmong during that time period, bounced from living in their villages to surviving in the jungle to existing in refugee camps depending on which location was safer at the time. The ultimate goal of his family and so many others was safe passage to a country of refuge, the United States, Canada, Australia or France. Unlike many immigrants, the Hmong did not desire a life in another country, nor did they want to leave their homeland. The death of thousands of their people, however, motivated this exodus across the world.

Shoua is the eleventh child of his father, Cher Poua Her, and his mother Mai Vang Her. With the Pathet Lao hunting them like animals, the clan fled their homes. While the next place of settlement was being determined by the elders, families such as Shoua's took refuge in temporary camps.

Mai (pronounced My) squatted over the stamped earth of their shelter, grunting and breathing in quick gulps. She did not scream during her labor, as childbirth is done quietly in the Hmong culture. (Medical providers who have worked in US hospitals with Hmong patients have described the difficulty in assessing pain levels in a culture where it is not commonly displayed. In this case, the mother, aunts and other older female relatives serve as invaluable resources for the Hmong women during delivery.) Shoua was born in the winter of 1961. His exact birthdate is unknown, as is the case for many indigenous people who live in harmony with the land and are not ruled by clock and calendar. If the family had practiced shamanism, they would have smeared blood and feathers from a sacrificed chicken along the side and top of the door after the birth to keep away evil. Wooden daggers would have been seen hanging from the bamboo door frame in order to "spear any intruding evil spirits."

Figure 3, Wooden daggers hang from a doorway to spear intruding evil spirits. Photo used with permission of Dr. Robert Cooper.

Shoua's mother gave birth inside of the family home, a privilege she enjoyed since she knew who the father was. (Hmong women who practice shamanism and who do not know who the father of their child is must deliver their babies outside of the family home in a bamboo hut built especially for the occasion.) Mai would have bound her breasts tightly after breastfeeding. In the old country it was believed that if the mother, while cooking and serving food to the family dropped any breast milk into either the family's food or the pig's food, she would be struck by lightning.

Mai ate only chicken, eggs and rice and drank hot water infused with postpartum herbs during the first thirty days after Shoua's birth (visitors after thirty days would have brought the customary gift of salt). Eating these foods, along with sitting by the fire to get back the heat believed to have been lost during childbirth, helped her gain back her strength and have enough milk for the baby. She wrapped her stomach to keep her back strong and wrapped her head, as exposure to any wind in the breezy Hmong house would cause her to have headaches when she was older. After that time she would be considered healed and ready to go back to working in the fields. Normally Mai wouldn't have left the house or have had visitors for those first thirty days in order to avoid both sickness and evil spirits, but an unusual event triggered her rapid departure.

Shoua was born in a small tent in a temporary camp in Laos where people relied on United Nations aid workers to deliver food and medical supplies. While families could occasionally grow vegetables in small gardens in the camps, they were mostly reliant on these thrice weekly deliveries from the UN for their food. Shortly after Shoua's birth, relief agencies were dropping emergency supplies from Dakota airplanes. The aid worker heaved sacks of rice out of the open door of the low-flying aircraft without examining where in the camp they might land. As the heavy bags were thrown to the ground below, the 50 kilogram (over 100 pound) sack came very close to landing on the flimsy shelter with infant Shoua and his mother inside. Shoua's mother, terrified that the next time a parcel was dropped they wouldn't be as lucky, ran out of the tent with her newborn baby. The family maintains that the shock and exertion from this near miss so soon after giving birth is the reason Shoua was the last child she delivered. Just days after his birth, Shoua experienced his first foray into near misses and survival.

There was very limited medical infrastructure in the camps. Baby Shoua was malnourished, sickly, and felt the stress of the adults surrounding him. When he was five months old, Shoua was in a coma induced by illness and fever. If the family had practiced shamanism they would have called in the shaman to deal directly with a spirit that may be angry or seeking revenge, causing the injury or illness in the victim. The family may have sacrificed a chicken or pig to trade for Shoua's soul, which seemed to have wandered from his tiny body. The spirit may have been appeased by this gesture and let the baby live. Shoua's family was Christian, however, and they called in the priest to bless the baby in case he didn't make it through the night. The priest told the worried parents and siblings that if they wanted the baby to live and have an opportunity at life, Shoua would wake up on the first cock crow (very early in the morning, before sunrise- around 3:00 am). If they wanted him to die and have an end to his suffering, he would do so at the first cock crow. Amazingly,

Shoua did indeed wake up at first cock crow and began crying. Shoua's parents breathed a sigh of relief as their baby had won another early fight for survival.

The majority of Hmong practice shamanism and animism, the belief that souls or spirits reside in nature, including objects and non-human animals. Before Shoua was born, however, a missionary from the Christian Missionary Alliance visited the village where Shoua's parents lived. The missionaries reportedly made the trek into the high mountains because they faced great resistance from the lowland Lao, who practiced Buddhism. As the missionaries climbed the hills into Hmong villages they were met by some clan elders who were interested in the teachings being offered. It is the clan leaders who make decisions for the village. Once the elders of Shoua's parents' village decided they preferred Christianity, it was decided that the village would become Christian. By the time Shoua was born, there was no question that he would be raised as a Christian. Even Hmong who had converted to Christianity, however, sometimes continued to practice their traditional shamanistic beliefs to keep evil spirits at bay. When one of the older cousins became ill, the family worried that the *poojong* (a devil, spirit or "little ghost", *poj ntxoog* in Hmong) would take over his body. To confuse the little ghost, Shoua's mother dressed the man in the skirts of a Blue Hmong woman so the *poojong* would not recognize the cousin. Later that evening, as Shoua's sister was boiling vegetables for the evening meal she noticed a stick of bamboo sticking up out of the pot. The sister wondered how the stick got in there and then concluded it was put there by the spirit, angry because her mom had helped the cousin. (Dressing him in women's clothing seems to have worked because the cousin did not die until 2014.)

The Her clan had moved to the relative safety of a temporary camp when the Pathet Lao had been raiding villages near their own. When the soldiers had moved far from the area to search for other Hmong, word trickled into the camps that it was safe to return to their village for the time being. Traditionally, Hmong communities didn't assign names to their villages. A village, therefore, was a loose collection of homes inhabited by (usually) related family members. If they had to refer to their village, the Hmong would cite a local geographical reference such as a nearby river or mountain, using the corresponding word in Thai or Lao, names people living in the lowlands would recognize. Using the Lao geography, then, Shoua and his family came from the Xieng Khouang province. The Hmong, though, used their own references. Shoua smiles as he explains that if he had been the first person to move to a mountain and he was a famous Hmong, that geographical area would henceforth be called, "Shoua's Mountain." If homes were built near lots of pine trees, the area might aptly be called Pine Tree Village. Another area was called Village of Ba, *ba* meaning "no trees". In this way, the Hmong demonstrate their connection with the earth and their physical surroundings.

Shoua's parents rebuilt their home using the traditional bamboo frame with a thatched roof made of banana leaves and hay. According to Robert Cooper's, *The Hmong; A Guide to Traditional Life*, if Shoua's dad had practiced shamanism he would have "dug a small hole in the spot where the main house post was to be erected, pile rice in the hole in the shape of a conical pyramid and cover the rice with an upturned bowl; this is left overnight. The rice would have been examined the following morning: if the pyramid remained intact, the house would prosper. If the pyramid had crumbled or partially crumbled, it was taken as a sign of spiritual displeasure which would manifest itself in sickness and death." Since many Hmong who had been converted to Christianity still practiced certain elements of their traditional ways, Shoua's dad may yet have done this.

The home would have had two fireplaces but no chimney; the smoke would curl around itself indoors. While many hill tribe people live in thatched homes raised by stilts, the Hmong build their homes directly on the ground, with stomped earthen floors. Corn is hung to dry from the high rafters in the house. The Hmong make smaller raised structures to keep rice, corn and other harvests off the ground and away from ants and other pests. Pigs seek out the shade of these small structures, squealing in the afternoon heat. Dogs and chickens roam freely in a constant search for something to eat. A rooster, or "judas cock" is kept tied to a branch up in a tree. He serves the dual role of alarm clock in the morning and also as a lure. The family would often take the rooster to the fields and tie it to a peg or secure its leg to the branch of a tree. His cries would sometimes attract curious wild chickens, and Shoua's father and the other men working in the fields would try to shoot whatever animals wandered into the fields in response to the rooster's calls.

Figure 4, A typical Thai village dwelling (Hmong structures are similar but aren't raised)
Photo taken by author

Figure 5, Contemporary picture of a Hmong home in Laos.
Photo courtesy of Shoua Her (used with permission)

Breakfast consisted of steaming hot rice and a thin vegetable soup eaten using Chinese spoons. Sometimes the family enjoyed noodles, made by pushing a paste of pounded, soaked rice through a sieve into boiling water. Afterwards, the family tended to the rice harvest. Mai kept baby Shoua either strapped to her in a hand embroidered apron-like cloth or within hand's reach as she worked. There are no babysitters or plastic baby carriers as there are in the west and babies go everywhere with their mothers.

Figure 6, Hmong baby carrier. Photo taken by author and used with permission from the Traditional Arts and Ethnology Centre (TAEC) in Luang Prabang, Laos

Figure 7, Children stay close to their mothers and caregivers. Photo used with permission of Dr. Robert Cooper

The family followed the traditional Hmong practice of slash and burn farming, entailing slashing down forest trees and other vegetation and burning it, creating nutrients in the soil. They would grow crops of corn, rice or vegetables on the land until the soil began to lose fertility then move on to another location and allow the forest to slowly reclaim the land. One of the major crops harvested in the region was rice. The Hmong are credited with being among the first people to cultivate the grain. It has been said in folklore that when farmers carry the rice home from a harvest, they are especially wary of dropping even a single grain of the rice into a stream because, "If the Lord Dragon sees some of our rice drop into the water, he will think we have more rice than we need and make it decrease." While many kinds of rice are grown in paddies which allow the farmer to use fertilizer and control water levels through irrigation, the Hmong lived in the highlands and grew 'upland rice'. This variety of sticky rice is suited to the terrain but tends to be a low-yielding subsistence crop. Shoua's parents and other rural farmers would climb the steep mountain to plant, weed, and harvest the rice, starting on the lower part of the slopes and working their way up.

Figure 8,   Rice is planted and harvested on very steep terrain. Photo taken by author in Hmong village near Luang Prabang, Laos

Figure 9,   Rice is thrashed over a split log then left
in the sun to dry. Photo taken by author in Hmong
village near Luang Prabang, Laos

Upland rice is planted on dry land on the steep slopes up the side of the jutting peaks in northern Laos. Once harvested, it is thrashed over a split log to separate the rice grains from the stalk, then laid out on sheets of plastic in the sun to dry. Rice is an essential crop in Southeast Asia and is incorporated into nearly every meal. The government of the Lao People's Democratic Republic (Lao PDR) is attempting to change the way some traditional farmers (including the Hmong) have cultivated rice crops. Lao PDR is developing policy to "stop shifting cultivation", which employs slash and burn farming techniques, in order to lessen environmental damage, protect watershed areas, and promote more sustainable farming practices.

In neighboring Cambodia during the beginning of the rainy season, a Royal Ploughing Ceremony takes place. "The King and members of the royal family perform the first symbolic ploughing lines in the royal rice field to prepare for the new crop. The ceremony is concluded with seven trays of food offered to oxen with rice, corn, sesame seeds, beans, grass, water and wine. It is believed that the food chosen by the oxen predicts the weather forecast and guides crop selection for the while year." Rice is essential to the Hmong community as well. At harvest time, Shoua and his siblings helped his parents climb the steep hillsides to gather and dry the rice so they could begin planting the next crop.

Poppies were another common crop grown by the Hmong. When Laos was a French colony in the 1940s, the French excised an annual "opium tax" on each Hmong household to help pay for road, market and airfield construction. It could be paid in silver, but many families paid with opium. Later, foreign buyers provided a steady market for the poppies to feed their hunger for the substance. The Hmong found themselves fighting a reputation for being drug manufactures (due to growing poppies for opium), destroyers of the environment because of their slash and burn farming methods and as insurgents of the government due to their part in the war.

Poppy flowers, grown to produce opium, grow best at higher, cooler elevations with rocky ground and low humidity. They are a cash crop. Raising animals for slaughter takes time and villagers couldn't raise the animals fast enough to make money. For a community that survives on subsistence farming, such a cash crop is vital. According to Anne Fadiman in *The Spirit Catches You and You Fall Down*,

> The Hmong.... knew how to choose the best soil for growing opium by tasting it for its lime content. They knew how to broadcast the poppy seeds in cornfields so the young plants would be protected by the corn stalks. They knew how to incise the pods with triple bladed knives (cutting neither so deep that the sap dripped to the ground nor so lightly that it was trapped inside the pods), wait until the extruded sap coagulated and turned brown, scrape it, wrap it in poppy petals or banana leaves, knead it and form it into bricks.... One kilo of opium was worth as much as half a ton of rice.

As the opium harvest falls at a different time from either corn or rice, the Hmong could harvest each of their crops one at a time. After a maximum of ten years of opium harvests, however, the land was useless for farming. No amount of time laying fallow would bring back the nutrients the poppies had leached from the soil. This contributed to the semi-nomadic lifestyle the Hmong practiced.

Traditionally, the Hmong used opium medicinally. Some swallowed it in pellets, some warriors mushed it into a putty and used it topically and others smoked it, usually while laying on their side. Opium was usually smoked when it was raw or in a semi-cooked form, "with a comparatively low narcotic content." In the absence of hospitals and medical providers, they utilized opium as a short-term treatment for illness and injury and to alleviate hunger pangs. They found it particularly effective for diarrhea, stomach problems, fevers and pain and as a sleeping aid for the elderly. Shamans smoked it to aid in their spirit travels and some Hmong deliberately overdosed on it when suicide seemed the only solution to the many traumas of life and war. While some villagers struggled with addiction, the use of opium was for the most part medicinal and an accepted part of the culture.

While his parents tended the fields, Shoua attended first and second grade in the village school where he learned how to write in Laotian, a skill he no longer possesses. Shoua was fortunate, as many Hmong children in Laos, especially girls, received very little education and few could read or write. When the Hmong lived in China, they were forbidden from using their own language. Hmong women attempted to preserve their symbols in embroidery, but the language was eventually lost and the Hmong practiced an oral history tradition instead. Literacy rates were different for other ethnic communities. The Lowland Lao created manuscripts on palm-leaf (and sometimes mulberry tree paper) from the mid 1500s until early in the 18th century. (To this day local artists paint on rice paper and parchment made from coconuts, banana leaves and even compounded elephant dung.) The Lao would make the so called "baylane" by cutting and boiling palm leaves and leaving them out to dry in the sun before writing script using an iron pen. They would then apply oil and black carbon. When the oil and carbon were removed, the writing remained. Interestingly, Lao Buddhists believed that if they ate a fragment of the parchment after it had been soaked in water, illness could be cured. The Hmong didn't have their own written language until a missionary developed one using Roman alphabet in the 1950s. To date there are still some Hmong villages in Laos where children don't attend school.

When he wasn't in class, Shoua was out in the woods with his friends and cousins enjoying a normal Hmong childhood, however brief. Armed with a knife, he hunted for mice, river frogs and other tasty treats, and wielded a slingshot or bamboo crossbow to bring down small birds that nested in palm trees. The benefit of a crossbow over a gun was its silence. If he shot at a bird and missed, he hadn't just frightened off every bird in the area with the sound. (It was also faster to reload than a musket and more reliable.)

Figure 10, A crossbow made out of bamboo Photo taken by author near a village outside of Luang Prabang, Laos

When he grew thirsty he used his knife to cut open bamboo for the refreshing water it contained. One day, eight-year-old Shoua was cutting a piece of bamboo when his knife slipped and he sliced his knee, creating a scar he bears to this day. He and his cousins threw stones into the rivers, chased little birds, rats and other wild animals, playing outside until it grew dark. They didn't need to be called in- no child wanted to be caught outside after dusk when the bobcats and tigers began their nightly prowl. Sometimes the children saw deep scratch marks a tiger had carved into the bark of trees or saw the large cat's telltale scat. In the evenings, the family could hear its deep roar resonating through the forest and reverberating through the trees. Villagers reported feeling more threatened by tigers before the war came to Shoua's village. The war brought guns, flashlights and hand grenades to the Hmong which changed the power balance of the jungle. The children were also wary of the *poojong*, described as the spirit of a fierce little girl who reportedly ran about the forest, unkempt and wild. Hmong folk tales are filled with stories of ghosts and of tigers who try to kidnap and marry girls and of people who have been transformed into tigers.

One day, munching on a beetle and scratching a mosquito bite, Shoua and his cousin were walking through the sun dappled forest dragging sticks to create designs in the dirt. Suddenly, the cousin jumped back, grabbing Shoua's arm painfully. "What?" hissed Shoua, startled. The cousin seemed frozen in place and raised his arm, pointing. There on the trail lay a pit viper. Bright green, it had a long, thin body, triangular head and beady eyes. The boys crouched down a safe distance from the snake and watched it slither through the leaves. Before it could disappear into the foliage, the cousin took the stick he'd been carrying and hefted it over his head, bringing it down onto the snake with a force belying the child's size. He struck the snake again and again, killing it. He then raised his makeshift club and smashed the snake's head until its body seemed to shudder. The boys had been taught that if you didn't crush the snake's head it would come back to life. They did this with every whip snake, golden tree snake, and wolf snake they encountered. They were fortunate in that they did not encounter a python during their forays into the woods, as they are also common to the area.

One evening the family made the long trek from the rice fields back to their home in the village. As they walked one by one on the dirt path through the dark jungle, Shoua lagged at the end of the line, tired from tending to the crops. Eventually he heard a distant "Boom.... Boom..." and recognized the sound as coming from a funeral drum. One man would carry the drum, the other would beat it in rhythmic intervals (Shoua's father used to be involved in the drumming ceremonies before he became Christian). The drumming helped the spirit of the dead during its journey home. Frightened of the eerie sound, Shoua ran ahead of several of the people in line until he was firmly ensconced in the middle of the group. Surrounded by his parents, siblings and cousins, he felt safe and protected.

Shoua remembers his mother as being a generous woman. Although she didn't practice shamanism as a rule, she would still occasionally burn hot peppers under the thatched house to ward off evil spirits when she was feeling unsafe. This practice had the added benefit of ridding the house of the rodents and snakes that would otherwise seek shelter in the elephant grasses. She taught her children how to pick wild mushrooms. While some families would cook them in rice to see if the rice turned red (indicating they were poisonous), she had a different method. She explained to her children that if the mushrooms grew on the ground they were more likely to be dangerous than ones growing on a tree. If insects ate the mushrooms they were probably ok, but stay away from the fungi that the insects won't eat. And if the mushrooms grow on soil that has been burned (in the slash and burn method), then it is most likely ok. A family in their village chose the wrong mushrooms on one occasion and became very sick from the poison. Shoua's mom gave them water that had been filtered through a certain type of dirt and was able to treat them. She also used day lily, smartweed, mugwort, mint and balsam in teas for medicinal uses for her husband and children.

Ethnobotany, or the study of people and their environments, demonstrates the ways in which cultures adapt to their natural surroundings. Forest dwellers learn to use the local trees and plants for everything from the construction of homes to broomsticks, from treating gastro intestinal distress to sunburn. In Shoua's village, natural herbs and remedies were administered to treat a wide range of afflictions including fever, headache and even malaria. Women concocted medicines from their natural environments to help with conception (especially for a healthy male child), and to treat kidney stones, jaundice and abdominal pain. Today, some of the remaining Hmong become licensed by the Ministry of Health in Laos, where it is "recognized as an official trade by the government". Despite acclimating to bureaucracy, healers still pray to their ancestors before collecting herbs to be used as medicine.

Bamboo was used by the Hmong to make their houses, the shelves in their thatched homes, and crossbows for hunting. Bamboo is a highly versatile plant. Part of the grass family, bamboo is one of the fastest growing plants on the planet with over 1,000 species. Some can grow up to one and a half feet a day to a height of over 100 feet in one season. The stalks and fibers are currently being used in a wide range of products, including surf, snow and skateboards, computer keyboards, coffee filters, sheets and towels, steering wheels, beer, wine and biofuels. Shoua even used bamboo as a toothbrush, working a piece until it produced bristles.

After a long day of working in the fields, Shoua's father rested on his mat. He was sterner than Shoua's mother, either by nature or circumstance, and tried hard to instill a sense of responsibility in his children. In the evenings he worked on a knife handle he had made of wood, smoothing the surface with the leaf of a fruit tree, rough like sandpaper. One evening Shoua was engaged in the practice of leaf blowing, creating music by holding a leaf to his lips and blowing air over it. His nephew commented, "Hey- you're pretty good!" Shoua's dad put down his leaf-sandpaper and looked sternly at Shoua. "You're just a tiny kid!" he said. "Why are you leaf blowing already?" Shoua's dad was referring to the tradition that usually accompanies leaf blowing- it is often a courting strategy, a way for boys and girls to communicate with each other. Shoua, naturally shy, did not try to leaf blow again for many years until his age was more suitable for courtship.

Figure 11,   Shoua posing with his parents and older sister
Photo courtesy of Shoua Her

In the evenings, Shoua's mother would gather with his aunties and older female cousins near a small fire, bent over embroidery as they sewed and chatted about local news and the events of their day. Occasionally, one of them would pause in her work to take a sip of water from the water bucket using a bamboo scoop. His father would sit with the male relatives by the main fire drinking tea and smoking tobacco from a bamboo water pipe. A pot bubbled over the fire with corn from the harvest, potato, banana trunk, pumpkin leaves, and the casing left over once the rice was separated from the stalk. These food items simmered over the heat all day and were reserved for the pig that would be sacrificed and eaten during the New Year's celebration. Maintaining a good diet ensured that the family would have a fattened pig for the most important occasion of the year. (The other pigs ate vegetables and whatever vegetation they foraged throughout the day. Pigs provided an important source of protein and their fat was used for cooking.)

Any feeling of community or normalcy Shoua had enjoyed in his village would not last. The family received word that the Pathet Lao were headed their way. This would be the last day Shoua would spend in his village home before fleeing into the jungle where they would pass the next two years in survival mode. Before any of the families fled, there would have been a meeting of clan leaders. No important decisions were made in the village without the leaders of several clans present, discussing the point of view of all males present until a decision was made. As it became clear that there was little hope of life returning to normal, clan leaders realized that their very survival was at stake. Families fled into the jungle before the communists could get to them. There were tales of entire villages being burned down by the Pathet Lao to flush out remaining villagers and prevent their return. The Hmong slipped into the jungle where their chances of survival were higher. They knew the terrain, the edible plants and possessed the toughness that had helped Hmong before them survive where others could not. It was in this atmosphere that many Hmong families were forced to flee their villages for the jungle.

People often conjure up a romanticized vision of the jungle, complete with swashbuckling heroes traipsing through foliage, swatting the occasional mosquito and being led by machete wielding guides. The reality is far less appealing; those mosquitos carry malaria and dengue fever, and the bugs, insects and snakes are numerous and sometimes deadly. Man, as is often the case, would prove to be the most terrifying danger in the jungle.

Chapter 3
On Watch

It was after the harvest when Shoua and his older cousin, Cher Doua Her, bedded down in the rice hay for the night. They were on watch, a responsibility twelve-year-old Shoua dreaded. Since his father was too old, one older brother had drowned and another was already involved in battle, it was Shoua's job to participate in the lookout every few weeks. The young men would walk about thirty minutes or so away from their encampments and watch for the enemy. If they spotted the Viet Minh or Pathet Lao, the boys would draw their fire, shoot, and then run away. Shoua and the other younger boys usually drew the first shift as it was easier for them to stay awake at that time and it was safer. The enemy usually came around three or four in the morning, so the more mature and experienced men took the later shifts.

Shoua and his cousin looked up at the stars, shivering in the cold night air. They had their Army backpacks with them, filled with ammunition and rice. Shoua used his pack as a pillow with the straps laid out ready to grab if he needed to run suddenly. Filled with dread, Shoua wondered if tonight would be the night he would encounter the enemy. He had been lucky so far. He held his brother's M-16 rifle close wondering, "Can my gun protect my life?" Just as he thought his nerves would get the better of him, his cousin distracted him with a story of a recent military exploit in which he had been involved. In their native tongue of Hmong, Cher Doua told him,

We were told we had to take the hill. It was hard to breach–there were so many enemy soldiers on top and the slope was tall and steep. We needed air support for this to be successful, so the US military sent a spy plane equipped with smoke rockets across the top of the hill–if it had flown around in a recon circle it would have tipped off the enemy as to what was about to happen. The little plane dropped smoke rockets, which guided the larger planes in for a bombing run. As the two Air Force jets came around for a second bombing run, one of the planes burst into flames. We couldn't tell if the plane had been shot down, was flying too low and hit something or if it caught fire when it tried to drop the bomb, but it had flames coming out of it everywhere. The other jet took off. Then all of the T-28s and Air Force jets came and bombed the hell out of that hill until the North Vietnamese left–there was blood *everywhere.* So, one of the commanders told us they wanted us to retrieve the body of the pilot that went down. He said that as a reward if we found the body we could keep the pilot's pistol and watch, which was some kind of special watch, I don't know. So we went searching for this American pilot whose plane went down in flames." Shoua nodded to show he was listening. He shivered, wishing it was safe to light a fire for warmth. He was grateful for his cousin's story to keep his mind from the cold and his terror of being on watch. His cousin continued.

We hiked down to the burned area and saw footprints of the North Vietnamese everywhere. We figured they were running from the madness of all of that shooting and, hopefully, they weren't looking for our guy. Nothing good would happen if they found him first. Anyway, the second day we're out looking and the wind blew from a different direction. I smelled this charred, burned flesh and it almost made me sick. I told one of the searchers about it and we pressed on a little further before we spotted some parachute flapping in the bushes. That led us further to the plane–the body was still inside. That poor guy was unrecognizable, he was so charred. We looked around a little to make sure we had the right fellow–sure enough, there was his watch–it wasn't working- and his pistol. The plane had hit the ground so hard that the barrel of his pistol was bent! We tried to get the body out, but it was so burned it couldn't be moved without a body bag. Somebody radioed in that we'd found the pilot and needed a bag. A while later, a little plane flew by and had to drop one since there was no runway on this steep hill. I don't know what the pilot was thinking because he dropped the body bag off too high and the wind caught that thing and carried it way off- there was no way we could have caught it! Where it landed was too dangerous for us to retrieve it and the body was too damaged for us to carry without a body bag, so we never were able to bring that guy out of the plane.

Shoua shook his head at the story, forgetting his cousin couldn't see his reactions in the starlight. He thought about what it would be like to be on a plane, especially one that was on fire and out of control.

The next morning Shoua heard the first cock crow, the Hmong time keeping expression that meant it was still very early (around 3 am). He arose after the second or third cock crow to gather wood for the fire. He could only pick up dead wood he found nearby, as cutting any timber created too much noise and might alert the enemy. He enjoyed the fire in the morning as it helped him to warm his bones, chilled from the cold, fireless night he'd spent in the high mountains of Laos. Shoua reflected on the questions his parents had drilled him about before he'd left for his watch. His mother, in particular, was always terribly afraid something would happen to him while he was out on patrol. "What will you do if you encounter the enemy?" she would ask.

"Shoot and run," Shoua replied, hoping he looked braver than he felt.

"What will you do if you get separated from everyone and got lost?" his parents queried. Shoua responded that he would stay with the leader but if he was alone he would look at the constellations and the location of the sun as it rose and set. Getting lost in the mountains terrified young Shoua. This was before the time of GPS and cell phones, so being caught out on his own would quickly become a life or death scenario. Besides the enemy, there were other dangers lurking in the woods, including tigers and king cobras and the distinct possibility that he wouldn't figure out which trail on which mountain he should take to get home. The constellation strategy was a good one, but it only worked on clear nights, and usually not at all during the rainy season.

The small group of boys and men only stayed in the same place for a day or two before moving on to patrol another area. They drank water from a stream when they became thirsty and cut bamboo stalks for the water within, if there was no stream nearby. The group shouldered their packs and prepared to march on. One man would walk alone up front, moving his gun from side to side as he looked for signs of the enemy. A second man would then follow, twenty or thirty yards behind. In this way, the first four men would progress, allowing enough space in between that if the North Vietnamese shot at them they wouldn't mow down the entire group. After the first four, the Hmong reasoned it was safer to travel in small clusters. Shoua and his cousin brought up the group of six near the back, nervously fingering the rifles that were nearly as long as they were tall.

Shoua's mom harbored certain beliefs to try to keep her children safe during this time of war. When Shoua's older brother was fighting on the front lines, she would not allow any of the siblings to prepare to cook meat by puncturing it with a bamboo stick. Instead, when they wanted to roast the meat for dinner they would splice a piece of wood halfway and wedge the meat in between the two connected pieces before placing it all over the fire to barbeque. If they had pierced the meat on the sharp sticks, she reasoned, then the bullets could get through her son's skin. In this way, she did what she could to keep her beloved children safe during crazy times.

Before he knew it, it was time for Shoua's watch again. He hunkered down in his foxhole, gun at the ready. Shoua drew his plastic sheeting around him to act as a poncho in the driving rain. Rain dripped from the leaves on the trees around him and pooled at his feet, creating a thick mud. Shoua spent the hour of his watch with his eyes wide, scanning the foliage, his heart in his throat. When his shift ended, he sank with relief. Shoua never encountered the enemy when he was out on patrol; often his cousins would have run-ins with the North Vietnamese during the week long lookout just after his, but he was fortunate.

Chapter 4
Life in the Jungle

Shoua dropped his pack and sat on the damp ground. The sun filtered through the tree leaves high in the canopy and shone in patches on the leaf-strewn jungle floor. Shoua leaned against a teak tree and plucked the leeches from his toes, grimacing at the sucking sound created. The blood suckers were an inch long and as wide as a chopstick. They would have fallen off on their own eventually, but he didn't want them to take any more of his blood before doing so. He waved away the insects buzzing around his head and breathed in the pungent scent of rotting leaves. A purple orchid grew near him, its colors vibrant in the surrounding forest. His stomach grumbled, a sound he was all too familiar with. As he stood and brushed off the dirt, Shoua noticed something glimmering in the small patch of sun. A giant orb spider had spun a web between two trees and lay waiting for its prey. The long-legged insect spanned over four inches across and seemed to hover in mid-air in its silky lair. Careful not to walk into the web, Shoua shouldered his pack and hustled to catch up with his family.

Shoua's family, like so many thousands of Hmong like them, was now surviving in the jungle. They enjoyed no permanent shelter, no sense of the community that was created in the village, and no harvest from their crops. (The Pathet Lao often waited until just before the harvest season to begin their bombing campaigns. This strategy was very effective in creating severe hunger in the Hmong the soldiers were seeking to exterminate.) Shoua and 200 members of his family spent two years in the jungle, moving from place to place to stay ahead of the Pathet Lao and Viet Minh. The family trekked across dusty fields during the dry season and trudged through water fields (wet rice paddies) during the rainy season. They pushed their way through fields of corn and soybeans. When they camped for the night, family members would walk the equivalent of three or four city blocks *around* the camp in both directions when searching for food or water, so no trail was left for those wishing to do them harm.

The family sought protection by creating a shelter built of two sticks stuck in the ground, covered with banana leaves to stave off the rain. During monsoon season, from July to October, it rains almost every day, up to twelve inches a month. Humidity is high. The family dug small trenches around the structure so the rains did not pool under their shelter. Shoua helped his father pull plastic sheeting over the banana leaves to act as an extra layer of protection from the wet. The roll of black plastic was supplied by the US government and helped keep the shelter dry. The plastic eventually shredded, however, and after a time the family huddled under only the banana leaves. Fat water drops landed on the children's faces, awakening them from slumber. The one advantage gained by running out of plastic sheeting was camouflage; from the back, the shelter blended in perfectly with its jungle surroundings.

Figure 1, This is the type of shelter where Shoua and his family lived when hiding in the jungle. Shoua was able to recreate this lean-to on his trip to Laos in 2015. Photo courtesy of Shoua Her

Shoua's parents placed leaves on the floor to make sleeping on the hard ground more tolerable. It was important to always have an exit available in case of attack, so the sides of the shelter were left uncovered in case they needed to bid a hasty retreat. A fire was built toward the front of the shelter, providing minimal relief from the biting cold of the mountain night air. Fires had to be built cautiously, however, as the smoke was a giveaway as to their location and would direct bombers to their camp. The family timed their cooking to avoid detection, building a fire either very late at night or very early in the morning when the light was soft and mists clung low on the mountains. Clothes were laid close to the fire to dry, making for a chilly evening. Their few belongings were kept in bags, ready to be grabbed at a moment's notice if there was danger and the family needed to run. Even cooking pots were placed in the bag immediately after use, just in case.

Shoua trudged through the wet, dead leaves carpeting the jungle floor. His clothes clung to him as the rain fell, relentless. The humidity weighed him down and the mosquitos nearly drove him to distraction. He stopped to mix a portion of dirt and bitter plant and positioned it on his septic arm, infected by the small biting flies that were making a meal of his extremities. The mixture brought him temporary relief. Shoua continued his search for something for the family to eat.

The family initially staved off starvation by eating whatever they could find. They fared better on the north side of the Mekong River as food more was plentiful than in the south (into Thailand). They ate nuts, wild mangoes, lychee and bananas in addition to fish, wild vegetables and rice. Someone would climb a tree to pick a sour fruit and throw it down for the family to share. Sometimes the family would get lucky and find the eggs of wild chicken, birds or ducks, which they roasted in the ground next to the fire. They ate whatever animals they could find, including monkeys, Marmoset rats, pangolin (which resemble aardvarks) and lesser mouse deer. They encountered mongoose, but the creatures were too fast for the family to catch. If they had been able to catch it, Shoua assures me, there would have been nothing left. He was even reduced to eating spiders, spearing them with a bamboo stick, peeling off the outer layers and roasting them over the fire. Hunger is a powerful motivator in expanding one's palate. One time a cousin caught a bobcat and the family feasted on it hungrily. This was not a meal they would have typically eaten if they had been living in their village where food was more plentiful, but they were living in desperate times. The only animal the family refused to eat was vulture. The bird exuded a terrible smell due to its diet of the flesh of dead animals, so it was very unappealing to consume.

Some Hmong have credited wild potatoes as having saved their lives. Children learned where to look to find cassava roots (also called yams). They would dig six to eight inches into the dirt before procuring the white, hairy tuber. The potato was quite sticky and could cause infections in the mouth when raw, but when cooked they became quite tender, like a regular potato. If cassava root is not cooked properly the cyanide poison on the exterior of the root can cause significant health problems. The naturally occurring toxin acts as a pesticide and tends to keep it from rotting. Shoua remembers becoming very tired of cassava roots, but it was all the family had to eat for a while. The root was responsible for the family's survival.

In desperate times, people are forced to eat creatures, bugs and bark to survive. The stress on Hmong parents to keep their babies fed and warm must have been enormous, especially in light of the fact that it was not just hunger and the elements families had to contend with; they were being actively hunted. Shoua has remarked that he wonders how the contestants on the television "reality" show *Survivor* would do if they found themselves having to live off the land in the jungles of Laos.

Most times it was unsafe to hunt by firing a weapon, as it would be a dead giveaway to the enemy as to their location. Instead, Shoua and his family devised traps using sticks. They cut wood the width of a finger and arranged it so that when the bird moved one of the sticks, the heavier piece of wood would fall and break the bird's neck. Using this method, they caught swallows, mountain bulbuls, woodpeckers, hornbills and even fish owls to eat. Shoua's favorite bird to catch was the buttonquail. Since it nested on the ground, they were easier to catch and Shoua and his cousins would play with it by tying a string around the bird's foot and walking it around before they actually killed and ate it.

Figure 2, This is the trap the Hmong used. When a bird, rat or other animal triggered it, the heavy branch fell and broke the neck. Photo taken by Shoua Her

The boys created false trails to lure small animals. Rats would think they had found a small path in which to run, but Shoua and his cousins would dig into the rat's hole, catching the rats by the neck. Other trails led to a rope that once triggered, killed the prey. The family devised nets made of bamboo baskets tied down with rock in order to catch fish in the streams. They used bird bones to lure their supper into the nets; once fish and crabs got in, they could not get back out. The family ate eel, large roasted grasshoppers, cicadas, and new leaves from poppy plants. If it was edible, it was eaten.

One afternoon, Shoua and his cousin were out in search of food. Crossing through a strand of pepper trees, they heard a noise nearby and froze. Terrified, they didn't move as they tried to determine where the enemy was. The cousin fingered his rifle nervously as they scanned the trees and grasses around them. After many tense moments, the sound came again and both boys shook their heads and stood up. It was a squirrel. The most frustrating part of the experience was that the cousin couldn't use the weapon to kill the squirrel for meat, as the sound would give away their location. On another hunting trip, the boys managed to catch a bird in one of their traps but before they could get to it the catch was stolen by a spotted linsang. The linsang, with the body of a weasel and the markings of a leopard, was adept at stealing the meals Shoua and his cousins caught for the family.

Shoua saw serow, (an Asian mountain goat) but was not able to catch any. People in Laos still eat them today. His cousin caught an Asiatic black bear once. They smoked the meat in the cooking area of the shelter in order to dry the bear steak, otherwise it would have spoiled. Drying the meat made it last longer and they carried it with them on the journey. One of the tastier meals the family enjoyed was bamboo rat. Markets in Laos still sell this delicacy.

While foraging for food with his brother-in-law (the husband of Shoua's sister, Pa), Shoua found a fresh mango lying on the trail. The brother-in-law practiced shamanism and believed that a person should never accept a piece of fruit, or eggs or other foods found on a trail as they are left there by ghosts trying to trap you. If you take the food, the ghosts have your spirit and you will die. Shoua picked up the fruit; his brother-in-law said sternly, "Leave it!" Shoua, fortified by both his hunger and his Christian beliefs, stubbornly replied, "I don't care!" and ate the fruit. The brother looked Shoua up and down with a "Let's just see what happens!" expression on his face as he waited for the terrible inevitable to happen. Shoua shares, a little smugly, "Nothing happened to me."

As time went on, however, food became scarce and the family's health reflected it. People began to look skeletal and enjoyed far less energy than they had previously. Their diet consisted only of wild potatoes and bamboo shoots that were more slender than the ones that grew closer to the village, supplying less sustenance. The continuous movement, fear, and enduring the near constant rains took their toll on the family. While everyone was thin and tired, it was Shoua's father who began walking noticeably slower. His skin had turned a sickly grey pallor and Shoua could make out the individual bones on his father's thin frame as he walked behind his dad. His father was breathing heavily and walked like a very old man. He had grown alarmingly emaciated and was struggling to keep pace with Shoua and his siblings and cousins. Shoua walked with his dad, who kept falling further and further behind the family group. Shoua then sprinted ahead, trying to reach the rest of his family before running back to check on his father.

Shoua's fear of being separated from his group in the jungle terrified him and he found himself spending more and more time ferrying back and forth between his father and the rest of the family. As his father's steps became heavier and more laborious, Shoua grew very concerned, fearing his father wouldn't be able to continue the long journey. Shoua shared his doubts with his mother, who sent him back immediately to check on his dad. When he backtracked through the family's faint trail and found himself once again walking painfully slowly next to his father, Shoua encouraged him to hurry up. "They'll leave us! Hurry, Dad! We have to get going." As he watched the maddeningly slow pace his father kept, he tried in desperation to think of ways he could help his father. Maybe he and his cousins could take turns carrying him? But with each new idea, his mind would always return to the same harsh reality. Without food, which no one had, his father simply would not make it. Shoua suddenly realized with a sinking heart that if he chose to stay with his father, who would obviously not survive the journey, he, too, would die. In that moment, he had to choose between loyalty- staying with his father to help and protect him- or his own survival. It was under these circumstances that twelve-year-old Shoua left his father and ran back to his cousins. He never saw his father again.

Shoua picked his way through the minefield to catch up with his mother and cousins, wiping the tears from his eyes. He struggled to balance his feelings- his strong need to survive against the guilt and concern over abandoning his dad. He wondered what kind of son leaves his father alone to die... and what kind of son embraces an early grave in the name of filial loyalty? He wondered what his mother would say when she heard the news of her husband's impending death, although he suspected that somehow she already knew. Would she be angry at Shoua? Or would she understand his impossible decision?

Alone with his thoughts, Shoua passed bamboo shelters that had long since been abandoned and were now home to scorpions, rats and mice. His thoughts were interrupted by a sound he had not yet encountered during his travails. As he made his way to one of the outlying shelters, he heard a noise he couldn't discern; a tearing, crunching sound. He rounded the bamboo cluster and was startled to see a tiger on the trail directly in front of him. The beast had a thick reddish striped coat and a white belly and was ripping into the flesh of a corpse. It turned, its enormous paws now at a 90-degree angle to Shoua. Shoua held his breath, unable to move. Fear rooted him to the spot even as a part of his brain screamed for him to run. The tiger spotted Shoua and hesitated. Its eyes seemed to look right through Shoua and the boy felt the air escape his lungs. His nerves taut and muscles tense, Shoua stood frozen in place and felt as if the world had shifted into slow motion. The tiger sniffed the air, its white and black tail twitching from side to side. It licked its mouth and then slowly turned towards the trees. The giant cat lumbered into the forest, leaving behind its meal/victim. Shoua crumpled to the ground, unable to move for several moments. The rush of adrenaline that had attacked his body made him feel physically sick, and he fought back a wave of nausea as he sat on the jungle floor. He focused on his breathing, willing it to return to normal so he could make his way back to his mother.

The only safe way back to his family- the route that was known to be free of landmines- was the path Shoua and the tiger had shared. Shoua tried to catch his breath- what if the tiger came back? What if it wasn't hunting alone? He had to pass by the bamboo shelter in order to stay on the path and catch up with his cousins. The boy avoided looking at the mangled body inside and tried to breathe through his mouth so he couldn't smell the rotting flesh. He wondered who the body had belonged to and if he had suffered before he died. He shivered as he thought what might have happened if he had left his dad a few minutes before he did. Shoua crept down the path, calling out to the tiger so he didn't startle it again, terribly anxious to rejoin the rest of his family.

Tigers have posed a threat to people living in this area before. There are refugees from a tribe known as the "Long Neck People" who live in the mountains of Thailand. Originally from Burma (now Myanmar), they were allowed into Thailand by the government because of their persecuted status, but are not allowed to settle below a certain geographical latitude. As a result, they live in bamboo huts covered by banana leaves and sell their beautiful weavings to visitors. They also tolerate photographs from tourists, bussed to a makeshift market near their village to see these exotic people firsthand. What makes this tribe so interesting are the women. They wear heavy bracelets and coils of metal around their necks, adding a ring at a time as they grow. The practice creates the illusion of having stretched their necks (thus the 'long neck people'). In actuality, the rings break the women's collar bone which causes their deformity. The rings were originally worn around the neck and wrists as these are the most vulnerable areas if attacked by a tiger. They now continue the practice with their daughters because of the fascination it provides tourists and the income that they bring.

Figure 3,   A young woman of the "Long Neck People" wears metal coils as she works on her weaving. Photo taken by author

Shoua caught up with the rest of his family, choosing to walk at the back of the line of relatives. He refused to make eye contact and avoided engaging in any discussion. He knew if enough time and distance passed from where he had left his father the less likely it would be that anyone would try to send him back. He wondered how much time his father had left and if he would suffer much. He fervently hoped the tiger had run far away and would leave his dad and any other stragglers alone. Shoua wrestled with his feelings of guilt and the relief of his own escape.

In the evening, Shoua and his family determined the safest place to make camp for the night. They decided on a hayfield that was surrounded by shrubbery. A cousin reported that the Pathet Lao had been reported in the area, so they moved carefully and were on alert. They snuck in, crouching down so they wouldn't be seen. The hay felt like sharp needles in their feet, causing pain with each step. They stayed very still and moved only when the wind blew. When the shrub leaves were moving, it was much more difficult for the enemy to see them so they made slow, painful progress, effectively hidden by the swaying stalks and leaves. When the wind stopped, they stopped otherwise any movement was a giveaway as to their location. In this way, they were able to crawl slowly away from the men who wanted them all dead. They bedded down; exhausted from their day of trekking and foraging for what little food they could scavenge from the land. Bellies still empty, it promised to be a long, cold, uncomfortable night.

In the morning, the family heard shooting. Just as they had done with the wind movement, they moved when they heard the guns go off because they could determine from where the sound was originating and scurry in the opposite direction. As soon as the firing ended, they lay in the field as if frozen, catching their breath, muscles tense, waiting for the next muzzle flash for an opportunity to gain ground towards safety. It was during one of these opportunities to run when Shoua's sister, who was carrying the young, thin Shoua on her back, leapt over a tree branch and fell. Unable to catch her breath, her mother supplied her with a few drops of urine to aid in her recovery. The Hmong belief in urine extends to using it on cuts to avoid infection (and washing the area afterwards) and as a means to resuscitate an unconscious person. His sister was able to continue the journey after the treatment.

In a place where the enemy is constantly on the lookout to shoot and kill, the hunted must develop skills and techniques to communicate and survive. The Hmong fashioned bamboo whistles to imitate birdcalls in the jungle to communicate with each other. This method was far safer than yelling in order to locate another member of the traveling party. Shoua would whistle a bird call before he left his hiding place as a way to say, "This bird is me". Interestingly, one person would only use the call of the male species of bird, and the other as the female. In this way, a man wouldn't accidentally shoot a son or daughter, mistaking the movement in the grass as a Pathet Lao soldier.

Shoua scratched his skin until it was nearly raw. The fleas were really getting to him and had settled on his skin, in his hair, and in the few articles of clothing he possessed. Because they had no access to soaps or detergents in the jungle it was very difficult to wash the irritating insects away permanently. There was a plant the family boiled that created a soap-like consistency and while it helped for a while, it was not strong enough to rid them of the external parasites. He tried to think of something else to distract himself from his physical misery.

One afternoon, several men from Shoua's village and a few of his cousins suggested Shoua go hunting for food with them. Shoua told his mother and sister he would be back later, hopefully with some dove or other meat for dinner. The women would stay behind, as Shoua's two-year-old niece might make noise and inadvertently give them away to the enemy. Shoua shouldered his Army backpack, discarded by an American soldier. Other Hmong had similar rucksacks or tied traditional woven baskets to their backs. Some even fashioned backpacks out of old rice bags. He adjusted the straps to better fit his small frame and grabbed his knife. He fell in line with the men.

When the hunting party of six had traveled quite a distance, the elder of the group stopped the march and gathered the men and boys together. He quietly explained, "We will not be going back". Shoua looked from the older men to his cousins, trying to understand what was being said. He didn't want to question his elders, but his brain was screaming with questions. "It's still light- we have time to find food and make it back. Why wouldn't we go back tonight?"

"We're not going back. At all." the older man said, patient with the boy's questioning as he saw the fear etched in Shoua's face. "If we go back we will all die. I know this is not easy, but it is the only way we can survive." With that, the elder shouldered his rucksack and began walking again. The other men and cousins fell in line. Shoua blinked back tears, his mind reeling. He swallowed back a lump of anger mixed with fear. If he had known this was the plan, he would have quietly told his mom to grab her backpack and come with them. He understood the little girl may have made a noise- but why hadn't they brought his mother? Would the women be ok? Would he see them again? Shoua briefly considered breaking from the group and running back for her, but he realized he must stay with the group for safety and protection. Running through the jungle alone was dangerous and wouldn't do himself or his mother any good. He could only hope that his family would be safe at their temporary camp and that they would be reunited in the refugee camp. Shoua welcomed the feeling of emotional numbness that eventually engulfed him as he concentrated only on the rise and fall of his footsteps.

That evening, the group of men and boys passed through the jungle into abundant farmland. It was late July and fruits and vegetables were ripening in the fields. They squeezed themselves between bamboo thickets to stay hidden and darted out in the open in search of food from one of the gardens when no farmer was in sight. In this way, they were able to procure cucumbers and watermelon which the group munched on in the safety of the bamboo thicket. Shoua sat quietly, overwhelmed with his feelings. When the group was busy walking or hunting, he could distract himself from his troubling thoughts. It was during these quiet and restful moments when the guilt and anxiety would creep into his mind, unbidden. He chewed slowly, looking up at the heavens as the first stars of the evening began to twinkle. He did not see the beauty of the sapphire blue sky or puffy clouds or hear the soothing sound of the bamboo swaying in the breeze. He saw only his mother's face in his mind's eye and the empty feeling in the pit of his stomach. Young Shoua had no way of knowing that he would never see his mother again. He hadn't even said goodbye.

Chapter 5
A Dark Place

Shoua stepped carefully, placing one foot directly in front of the other. He focused on the bruised grasses from his cousin's steps in front of him, mindful to stay in the path his family had created. They resembled a line of picnic ants, never straying far from the person in front of them. To stray from the path could mean death. As Shoua negotiated his way through the minefield, he tried not to think about what would happen if anyone in his family miss stepped. He had heard about people being either killed or dismembered depending on what kind of mine they stepped on. One went off and exploded, immediately killing the unfortunate victim who'd triggered the ordinance. Another type wouldn't kill the person outright but would cut off their feet. The third mine, once activated, jumped 5 to 6 feet high before spinning and exploding, exacting a much bigger death and injury toll. Shoua wiped the sweat from his brow, concentrated on the foot placement in front of him and tried not to think about much else.

Figure 1, Map of Historical Records
1965-1975

According to the traveler's guide Lonely Planet, "By the 1973 ceasefire…Laos had the dubious distinction of being the most bombed country in the history of warfare". There were more bombs dropped in Laos (the size of Idaho) than in all of WW II. It is estimated that between 1964 and 1973, US armed forces flew 580,000 bombing missions over Laos, the equivalent of a bomb run every eight and a half minutes, twenty-four hours a day for nine years. Bombs were dropped by the US military in an effort to disrupt North Vietnamese supply lines and troop movements along the Ho Chi Minh Trail. Bombing runs were made by the US Air Force, US Navy, Marines, Army, and Air America (run by the CIA), Royal Thai Air Force and the South Vietnam Air Force.

Figure 2,   Remnants of ordinance Photo taken by author, courtesy of the Minnesota History Center, "We Are Hmong" exhibit

Cluster bombs are devastating. Some were designed to open in midair, the two clamshell-like halves opening to disperse more than 650 individual bomblets; each bomblet projected 300 ball bearings at ballistic speed, covering the surface area of three football fields. Others were designed to survive the impact of landing and become landmines.

According to information gathered by COPE, the Cooperative Orthotic & Prosthetic Enterprise located in Vientiane, Laos, unexploded ordinance (UXO) is defined as "all munitions and mines that have explosive, incendiary, and pyrotechnic or gas filling which have not yet functioned as they were designed". This continues to be a huge problem in Laos with an estimated one third of the country contaminated with UXO and an average of one hundred casualties every year. There have been over 20,000 Lao civilians (40% of those being children) killed or injured by landmine ordinance since 1973. Civilians, who are 98% of recorded cluster bomb victims, encounter bomblets through a variety of circumstances. Some find them while gathering items in the forest, working in gardens, rice paddies or tilling their fields for farming. In a country as economically poor as Laos, collecting and selling scrap metal can be fairly lucrative, especially when a primitive metal detector can be purchased for as little as $10. Rural families search for shell casings and bits of metal and transform them into everyday objects. Cups and serving spoons are created by beating cluster bomb cases, and cowbells are made from mortar shells. One creative family transformed large shell casings into stilts to support their bamboo home.

Figure 3,   Photo taken by author with permission at the COPE Visitor Centre in Vientiane, Laos

An amputee formed the tip of his homemade wooden leg with the same type of shell casing that was responsible for taking his leg in the first place. Because many household items have been created using scrap metal from UXO, children have grown up seeing it and fail to recognize it as dangerous. The search for scrap metal places both adults and children at risk of encountering one of the estimated 80 million unexploded 'bomblets' scattered throughout the Laotian countryside. During vegetation clearance to build up infrastructure in Boualapha District, a bulldozer uncovered dozens of UXO in the earth including an unexploded 500-pound bomb. It was very fortunate the ordinance was discovered before tragedy struck. One family wasn't so lucky; they lost four children and had another three injured when they built a fire in their yard on a chilly evening. They had no way of knowing that under the place they'd chosen for their bonfire lay an unexploded bomb.

Figure 4,   A field filled with unexploded ordinance Photo recopied with permission from COPE, Vientiane, Laos

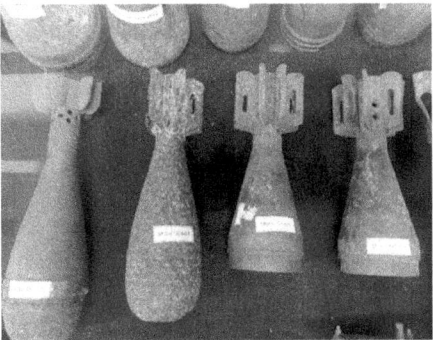

Figure 5,   Mortars dropped over Laos Photo from Lao National Museum, Vientiane, Laos

It takes specialists ten days to clear one hectare (approximately one and a half professional soccer fields), and even longer if the site is located on a hill or covered with vegetation. The ordinance must be cleared manually after being located with metal detectors. Once a bomb "is located, it is marked with a flag and prepared for demolition. Where possible, explosive devices are blown up where they are found."

For amputees, learning to walk with a prosthetic leg can be very challenging. This is especially true for rural Lao who live in traditional villages where homes are built on stilts. It is considered bad luck to live in a home with an even number of steps, and thatched houses usually have at least three (or five, or seven steps depending on how high the house is raised from the ground). Negotiating stairs, especially on uneven rough-hewn surfaces can be difficult, and even more so using ill-fitting, homemade wooden legs. COPE specializes in educating the public about UXO and provides cost effective, comfortable prosthetics for amputees in Laos. Since some of the survivors choose to become UXO clearance operators after learning how to live life as an amputee, COPE offers prosthetics made only from composite materials. With no metal components in the limbs, there is no interference when working with metal detectors.

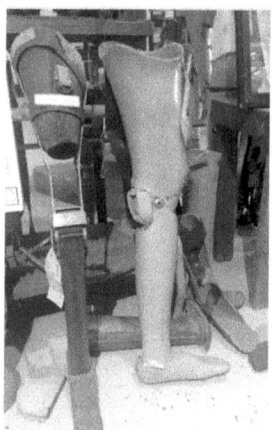

Figure 6,   Various prosthetic limbs have been used over the years as a result of limb loss caused by mortars and landmines.

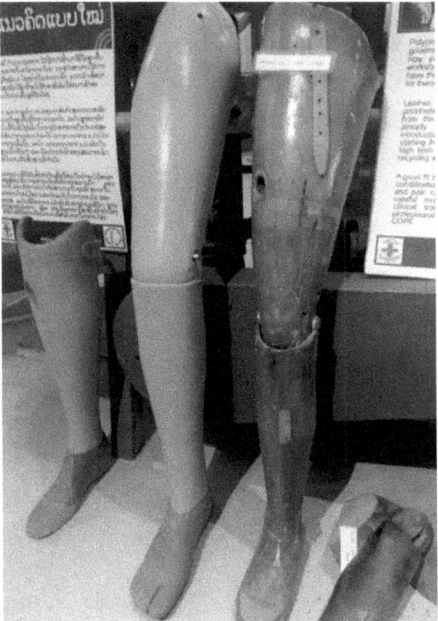

Figure 7,   Various prosthetic limbs have been used over
the years as a result of limb loss caused by mortars and
landmines. The leg featured above on the right is homemade. The middle one has been fashioned by COPE.
They are able to make prosthetic limbs for only $75.

Figure 6 & 7 Pictures taken by author with permission at
COPE, Vientiane, Laos

In a night market in Vientiane, the capital of Laos, booths
offer a variety of items - tee shirts, hand sewn wall hangings
and squid served on bamboo skewers. One vendor sells trinkets
made from the scrap metal of old ordinance. Spoons and key
chains are available in an ironic mix of forms, including small
hand grenades, bombs, flowers, and crosses. A display sign reads,
"Make Spoons Not War" and goes on to add that proceeds go
towards the development of the village through their community
fund. All of this takes place a few miles from COPE's facility
where they urge visitors not to buy such items. Purchasing these
trinkets encourages villagers to scour for scrap metal in the form
of ordinance, quite literally putting them at risk of life and limb.

Figure 8,   These key chains are made of old ordinance. Buying them
encourages villagers (especially children) to search for scrap metal which puts
them at risk for exposure to unexploded ordinance.

Photo taken by author at night market in Vientiane, Laos

Not all of the bombing in Laos was done by the American,
South Vietnamese, and Thai forces. Mortars were dropped on the
Hmong by the Pathet Lao as their efforts at genocide escalated.
During the bombing campaign, caves played an interesting role
for both sides of the conflict. Southeast Asia paints a dramatic
landscape of jagged peaks covered with vegetation and thick mist.
Hidden within the limestone mountains are enormous caves,
some spreading underground for more than a football field in
length. The Pathet Lao reportedly detained Hmong and other
prisoners of war in caves until the prisoners were taken to seminar
camps. The Pathet Lao (a minority of whom were Hmong) used
a cave in Viengxai as political headquarters until 1975 when the
Americans were trying to "bomb them back to the Stone Age".
The Pathet Lao and Vietminh created entire living and working spaces in the caves' interiors including makeshift hospitals,
cinemas, meeting rooms, bomb shelters, homes, weaving mills,
printing presses and workshops.

Figure 9,   Communists hid in caves, featured here in
Viengxay cave, Huaphanh Province
Photo from the Lao National Museum, Vientiane, Laos, used
with permission.

After 1975, some Hmong hid on Phou Bia and other high
mountains and in the caves of the craggy limestone cliffs for protection against the bombing by the Pathet Lao/Vietminh. Discussing
Khammouane Province, "The area was so heavily and consistently
bombed that whole villages were forced to evacuate the district,
those who could not or would not leave their homes sheltered in
nearby caves. In 2012, the area is still highly contaminated with
unexploded remnants of war, the most prolific of these are cluster
munitions. While traveling through the area, it was not difficult for
the WWM (World Without Mines) team to imagine the thunderous
sounds of explosions ricocheting off the limestone cliffs that create
the natural funnel of the Ho Chi Minh Trail."

Lowland Lao used the caves to keep safe their sacred objects
and artifacts; a number of caves have been discovered that con-
tain hundreds of Buddhas put there to protect them during
the bombings in the 1970s. Villagers would trek many miles in
order to safeguard their icons. Some of the Buddhas are made

from brown tree resin, others from champa wood, clay, concrete or iron. There are even some made of aluminum suspected of coming from downed US planes.

The North Vietnamese used the caves as an offensive weapon when they did the unthinkable. According to Keith Quincy in *Harvesting Pa Chay's Wheat*, "…after several days of hard fighting, the guerillas broke and ran, leaving behind three thousand Hmong, Lao and Khmu villagers who had been providing them aid. The Vietnamese herded the civilians into a cavern, blocked the entrance with logs, and fired chemical weapons into the cave. A handful of Hmong in the back of the cave survived the gassing, crawled out over the dead bodies, and escaped."

Figure 10, The caves were large enough to support this rally
Photo from the Lao National Museum, Vientiane, Laos.
Used with permission

In a fascinating twist, these beautiful mountains were used both offensively and defensively during the war, for protection and detainment, murder and salvation. An unsuspecting visitor would never guess the fear, hope, or tragedy felt deep within the towering limestone cliffs.

Shoua recalls that he and his family members were the intended targets of bombing runs often during their time in the jungle. He witnessed people getting hit with shrapnel and children with their faces blown off. The sound of artillery fire haunts Shoua to this day. He can talk about many memories of traumatic events calmly but the recollection of artillery fire and incoming mortars causes him to tear up as he talks. He describes the sound: "like a cat- "Mrrrrrrew" as it goes on either side of you. If you hear nothing right after it fires, you're in trouble, as it's coming *at* you." Shoua's cousin sat with him by the fire one afternoon. The cousin got up to retrieve something and within seconds a fragment of metal from artillery landed exactly where she had been sitting just moments earlier. The fear in their bellies far outlasted the ringing in their ears and the curling smoke from the ordinance.

Shoua dug in the hard ground, rooting for the wild potato he knew would grow there. His fingernails were dirty and ragged and his shoulders ached from the effort. Then he heard it- the low rumble followed by the whine of the engine. He screamed a warning to his cousins and broke into a run through the foliage. The plane would be overhead soon, flying low over the treetops. Shoua wasn't sure if it was on a scouting mission or a bombing run, but he didn't want to find out. He ran until he thought his lungs would burst, feeling very exposed and vulnerable. Finally, he reached a rock outcropping and he threw himself under it just as he heard the whistle of the mortars emanating from the plane. Some of the mortar fire came from planes the US had abandoned when they left Laos. The planes originally held smoke rockets intended to mark the position of the enemy for the aircraft that followed with bombs. The enemy converted the abandoned aircraft; instead of holding two rockets under each wing, the planes now had a five or six rocket capacity under each wing. The planes, in their search for Hmong exiles, shot rocket-propelled grenades that yielded a thick smoke which drifted and clung to the mountainside. Shoua heard gunfire every day and recalled CIA spy planes flying over day and night. He spent the night praying that if a mortar hit, it would hit behind him where he was protected by the rock, not in front of him where he lay exposed. The mortar attacks were terrifying- great chunks of earth exploding, dirt raining down all around, the air filled with dust and the screams of the wounded. Out of habit, parents tried to shush their children who cried out in terror and confusion. Frightened little ones buried their heads into the skirts of their mothers. The young ones didn't understand why the planes were searching for them, hunting them down as a tiger seeks out a water buffalo. No amount of elders' wisdom could explain why the planes were firing rockets in the hopes of destroying them.

Chapter 6
Crossing the Mekong

Shifting his weight from one foot to the other, Shoua strained his neck to see above the crowd. Surrounded by thousands of nervous people hoping to cross the Hin Heup Bridge to safety, he could sense the mixture of sweat, fear and anticipation that mingled in the shimmering heat. His cousin motioned for Shoua to stop fidgeting- it might bring the soldiers' attention to the family and the attention of the Pathet Lao was the last thing the family needed. Shoua grimaced in frustration at the family's position in the crowd. Near the back, they may not get the opportunity to cross before the soldiers closed access to the bridge.

The year was 1975 and American fighters had left Laos. Hmong were being rounded up and taken to concentration camps. The Pathet Lao also used the strategy of making a presence in Hmong villages to enforce the laws of the new communist government. Once the troops had won the trust of villagers, the Pathet Lao would work to uncover who had fought with the CIA and Hmong warrior, Vang Pao. Those interviews would lead to executions. The Hmong in Shoua's province knew that sooner or later the Pathet Lao troops would begin to infiltrate their communities. The time had come to elude the soldiers before the penetration into the villages could begin.

The options to flee from Xieng Khouang province to Vientiane were limited. At that time, the escape route required families to pass through the gates of two different bridges crossing large rivers. Shoua's family, alongside hundreds of other frightened Hmong refugees, broke through the gate of the first bridge at Na Su and traveled several weeks more to reach their second obstacle, the gate at the very long, narrow Hin Heup Bridge. The families prepared to break down the gate to this bridge, much as they did at Na Su. Since this was the only local bridge that spanned the river, thousands of families were funneling towards the main gate, yearning to cross to Vientiane and eventually to Thailand. Rumors were spreading that the Pathet Lao were starting to prevent people from leaving Laos and may be closing access to the bridge- this may be the last opportunity to cross to safety. Soldiers were carefully checking each traveler and asking menacingly, "What do you do for a living? Are you involved with the CIA?" The number of families from surrounding villages pressed together, hoping to get through the checkpoint.

As more and more desperate families lined up to cross the bridge to safety and freedom, the soldiers grew increasingly anxious and hostile. The soldiers' eyes grew wide as the influx of fleeing people grew and created a frightened river of humanity. The Pathet Lao lowered a barricade across the bridge entrance and yelled at families to go back to their villages because Laos was now at peace and this was a "liberated zone", a communist euphuism for a region they now controlled. Tensions mounted as families pressed forward, sensing that their window of opportunity for escape was narrowing. Parents held their small children and grasped the hands of their elderly parents, intent on taking this opportunity to cross to safety. Soldiers fingered the triggers of their M16 rifles and shouted for families to back away from the gates. Then, in a horrible moment, they opened fire. The noise of the gunfire mingled with the smoke of the mortars they fired into the crowd. Shrill screams erupted from terrified family members as their loved ones collapsed around them, grasping bleeding limbs and chests.

Shoua and his family were at the back of the line about a half mile from the bridge's gate. They turned and quickly fled back into the jungle. The family had felt unlucky to have been so far from the bridge entrance, yet that turn of events had saved their lives. They ran deeper and deeper into the woods until they felt safe enough amongst the eucalyptus trees and bamboo thickets to stop and catch their breath and recover from the adrenaline dump their bodies had just experienced. Shoua and his family looked at each other as they gasped for air, stunned. Had the soldiers really just opened fire on innocent people trying to cross the bridge? Had they just been spared because of their place in line? Wearily, they decided to hike further into the jungle, just in case their location had been betrayed somehow. Villagers ran back to their homes to dig up the weapons they had hidden.

Later on the same day of the massacre, Shoua's older brother Vang heard that the bridge had been reopened. He and his wife left to investigate. Sure enough, because the massacre had proven so effective in scattering and terrifying the multitudes, soldiers had moved on to patrol other areas and Shoua's older brother and sister-in-law were able to cross to safety. Shoua often wondered why Vang never returned for him and for his parents and siblings. The bridge was deemed unsafe for travel after that day, and Shoua and his remaining family would be forced to cross the river the hard way.

Under 1970s communist rule, the Mekong River had been compared to the Berlin Wall of Germany. As the natural border between nations, it served as the barrier between Laos and Thailand, between death and freedom. This is no symbolic creek- the mighty river is one of the twelve largest in the world and flows for thousands of miles, its volume increasing seasonally with snow melt and monsoon rains. Hmong who practice shamanism believe that the rains are controlled by a dragon named Naga; the amount of rain directly affects the amount of water flowing through the Mekong. (There is an interesting parallel in Japanese culture. It was said that a dragon king lived in the imperial garden in Kyoto, Japan. Buddhist monks held ceremonies during times of drought to persuade the dragon king to rise and bring rain.) The Hmong have called the Mekong the River of Death because of family members swept up in its swift currents. This is the very river Shoua and his family had to cross to freedom.

The men who work as border patrol in Laos are employed by one of the poorest countries in the world. Some families wanting to cross were fortunate and "knew a guy" and were able to pay a bribe to the border patrol to ensure their safe passage across the mighty river. Other refugees crossed via canoes led by Thai smugglers. Scores of others, however, were less fortunate. They had to attempt the crossing themselves and either drowned or were shot and killed during their attempt to cross. It was difficult to determine which was the greater threat; starvation, the gun-wielding soldiers on patrol or crossing the mighty river itself.

To get to the river and rejoin the rest of the family, Shoua and his cousins followed the "highway", a dirt road running north to south. The boys waded through several rice fields during their journey. Because it was the rainy season the water in the paddies was high and Shoua, a small statured boy to begin with, could barely see over the tops of the plants. He listened attentively, preparing to dive and lay down flat in the water if someone came out shooting. He breathed in short huffs as he strained through the murky water. They exited the paddy and jumped over a log- Shoua landed in a heap of elephant dung. Suddenly, he felt a sharp pain on the bottom of his foot. There was no time to explore the cause of the discomfort- he had to keep moving. He now shuffled with a noticeable limp, however, and began to lag further and further behind. His cousins kept whispering, "Hurry up! They'll shoot us!" With his cousins running, Shoua limped through the next rice field. Struggling to keep up, Shoua followed his cousins as they passed through another field and village, staying hyper vigilant of any dogs, farmers or armed soldiers who may be nearby. They eventually made it to the area of the Mekong they planned to cross, located on the far side of the busy road. They hid in the bushes the entire day, sharing space with a colony of ants. Shoua wasn't sure if they had inadvertently disturbed the ants' nest or if the boys, in their cadaverous state, smelled like death and the ants had come to feast. Either way, the boys slapped their thin arms and scratched the tiny bites as they hid. They lay in hiding from morning until 8:00 pm, waiting for traffic to die down and darkness to settle in. With no flashlight (any light would give away their location) they crept along near the road, avoiding detection. The boys followed the sound of traffic. If it were silent they knew they were headed in the wrong direction. Noise meant humanity and eventual freedom. When they needed to cross the road, they waited until it seemed clear before two of the boys would run together, dive into the long grass and wait. If no car came by, another two made a break for it, then another pair. When they all gathered together on the far side of the road, they lay panting, listening for anyone who may have spotted them. The fear of hearing the sound of a machine gun haunted them all. Dogs barked in the chilly night air, spooking the boys. Once they had caught their breath, the boys shimmied away from the road and stood up, heading down to the riverbank. They had reached the shores of the first river they must cross.

The boys needed to be wary as they approached the family's campsite near the river, as there were secret agents working as farmers who were paid to catch people trying to either escape or work against the government. While it sounds as though this would make it difficult to know who to trust, the truth was far simpler; trust no one. Soldiers on the banks of Laos would shoot someone because they were trying to escape. Soldiers in Thailand would call the UN because they didn't want refugees flooding into their country. As one survivor recalled, "On one side of the imaginary line separating Laos and Thailand, Hmong were citizens unwanted; on the other, we were refugees unwanted". Under these conditions, a healthy sense of paranoia meant a better chance of survival.

One evening as the family was eating grass and drinking boiled water for their daily meal another group of Hmong travelers passed them. "You need to move!" they cried. "They [the Pathet Lao] are headed this way!"

Shoua's family quickly packed up their belongings and slipped into the tall grasses. His sister Chue held her infant daughter Bao (pronounced Bo) to her breast, desperately hoping she would remain quiet. The baby was awake, with wide brown eyes taking in the scene unfolding before her. Her thin legs were beginning to kick, however, a sign that she would soon be getting fussy. A relative sought out an uncle, a known opium user, and begged him for a small amount to give to the baby. The relative hurried it over to Chue, who placed a few drops in water and fed it to her infant daughter. Chue knew of other families who had done this and their babies had become so listless that they stopped moving and breathing altogether. Chue didn't like taking the risk, but she knew if the little one cried out the entire family would be shot and killed. She tried to smile at her baby through her own tears as she coaxed the drug into Bao's tiny mouth. "Shhhhhhh….." she crooned, rocking her gently. Someone gave the signal for quiet, and Chue lay in the tall grasses with her baby, hoping the soldiers would sense nothing amiss and continue on their journey. Chue sensed her baby's body relax against hers and felt the baby's warm breath slow against her neck. She was impatient for the Pathet Lao to pass the field where her family lay hiding, so she could check on Bao and make sure she hadn't taken too much opium. The family was lucky–the patrol did not venture close enough to their area to spot anything and they remained undetected. Little Bao was also lucky. The dose of opium only quieted her and put her to sleep. Many families inadvertently killed their babies with this practice, but it was considered a risk worth taking while in the danger zones because if the babes cried out, the entire family would be massacred. Other women make the heartbreaking choice of leaving their babies behind in the care of family members staying in Laos, fervently hoping they would be reunited one day when the war was over.

The families hid quietly until the danger had passed. When it was safe, they slowly arose, stretching stiff bodies and breathing deeply. Mothers gave children some red banana blossoms (the red flower that grows on top of the banana bunch) to eat as the family prepared to move on in the opposite directions of the soldiers.

Families hoisted packs on their backs and began once again their trek through the foliage. After several hours had passed, one mother struggled with the weight of carrying her toddler, who had grown heavy in her arms. The woman inherently knew that the child could not walk the distance required and that she could not physically carry him anymore. Survival requires brutal choices that cannot possibly be understood in times of peace and bounty. The mother wrapped the small child in layers of clothing and placed him gently beneath a tree. With tears on her face, she desperately hoped he would be found by a loving family who could care for him, as she simply was unable to do now. She turned away and quietly joined the families streaming through the woods on their journey to the Mekong.

Many people drowned trying to cross the Mekong River. Few Hmong know how to swim, as Hmong mothers who practice shamanism teach their children never to enter deep water where the evil river spirits pull swimmers down. Interestingly, in Japan children are also warned to be careful when swimming in rivers and ponds because there is a creature called Kappa who will drag them under and drown them. Parents in Japan throw cucumbers, a favorite treat of Kappa, into the water as gifts so the monster would spare their children.

Hmong families used desperate measures to cross the river to freedom, including blowing air into plastic bags and tying them onto their arms. Some used banana tree trunks or bamboo to fashion flotation devices or rafts. Rafts can come apart in the rough currents, though, dropping its passengers into the turbulent waters. Perhaps for this reason, Shoua's family chose to use life jackets instead of bamboo. This meant that some of the cousins had to make a harrowing journey across to Thailand to purchase life vests while the rest of the family spent an entire month waiting and surviving in the jungles of Laos, near the bank of the river. In retrospect, Shoua laments this choice made by his family. He reasons that if they had cut lengths of bamboo (to use as floatation devices, much like the "noodle" found in many US swimming pools), lives would have been saved as family members died of starvation during the long wait. At the

time, however, life jackets seemed the safer choice by the elders
who made the decision for the family.

The cousins travelled to Thailand and begged family members living inside the refugee camps for money, who in turn
requested the money from family members already living in the
United States. This was not a matter of a simple wire transfer. In
those days, people in the camps would mail a letter to relatives in
the US, pleading for help. The family stateside would then send
cash. This process could take months. When the money finally
arrived, the cousins used it to buy floatation devices and finally
returned to their waiting family in Laos. There they discovered
that many elders had died of starvation during the wait and the
rest of the family was struggling to find enough food to survive.
The climate was drier here; no bananas grew, the bamboo shoots
were smaller, and wild potatoes were scarce. While the Mekong
was home to catfish, cob fish, and freshwater anchovies, throwing
nets or fishing line near the shoreline was risky, as border guards
kept a sharp eye for refugees. When the rainy season had ended
and the Mekong and other smaller rivers were no longer swollen
in size, some families were lucky and found fish still flopping in
rice fields, left behind by the receding waters. In some of the
minor streams, men created a small dam to funnel water through
a bamboo net. Fish that were upstream found themselves trapped
inside as the water levels dropped at the end of the rainy season.
Hunting for land-dwelling creatures was trickier. Shooting an
animal for food was out of the question as the gun report would
draw the attention of the border guards, although Shoua did
hear about a group that had come before them that somehow
managed to bring down an elephant and eat it- bone marrow
and all. "With no salt", he added.

While they were waiting for their cousins to arrive with the
life jackets, Shoua and his cousins ventured to a farm to scrounge
for whatever food they could find. They encountered a field
with rows and rows of small green plants with fat soybean pods
dangling under the leaves. Desperate to feed themselves, the
boys waded into the sea of green, ready to harvest some of the
succulent vegetables. As they bent down to pick the beans, the

farmer came running towards them, yelling for them to get off of his land, *right now!* In an effort to protect his crop and property, the farmer was wielding a large knife and thrusting it forward menacingly. Shoua raised the M16 rifle he had inherited from his cousin and pointed it at the farmer, trying not to shake or otherwise show his fear. The farmer abruptly stopped running and held up his hands–still holding the knife, but clearly without the intent to get close enough to use it. He shook his head angrily as the boys stuffed their pockets full of beans and ran off, turning around every so often to make sure they weren't being pursued. When they'd reached a safe distance, the boys stopped to catch their breath. Shoua found he was still shaking. His cousin asked in a husky voice, "Would you have actually shot that guy?" Shoua merely shrugged. He couldn't put into words all of the thoughts and feelings streaming through his mind. He had asked himself the same question. Sure, if the farmer was about to hack them to pieces with a machete, he would have felt justified in shooting him. But would he have been willing to kill a man over a pocketful of beans? Had he become so desperate? He stood and began to walk back to the encampment. He realized such questioning was irrelevant when his family, who was slowly dropping off due to starvation, was waiting on him, depending on him. He shouldered the rifle and walked on.

While it may seem shocking that a boy was carrying such a weapon, many Hmong families at that time had similar protection. It was not unusual for families to possess an M16 or similar rifle, at least one grenade and other armaments that they had used during the war, all supplied by the CIA. The rifles were often carried by the men as they crossed the Mekong River for use as protection in Thailand. Later, as ammunition and weaponry became scarcer, men would make grenades from gunpowder wrapped in leaves, with the fuses carried separately. Decades earlier the Hmong made their own grenades by mixing charcoal and sulfur with nitrates distilled from bat guano.

At one point the boys had to cross a river on their journey towards the larger Mekong. They waded across the murky waters, brown bubbles swirling in the eddies. While the river posed less of a challenge than they would soon face, it was an exhausting afternoon. When Shoua and his cousins reached the other side, they sat down to pick off the leeches from their skin. These leeches were bigger than the ones in the jungle, about the size of a man's thumb. The boys knew they needed to find something to eat in order to maintain enough strength to continue on. They had been expending far more calories than they had consumed and while they didn't think in those western terms, they knew instinctively they couldn't go much further without fuel.

The boys made their way into a bamboo grove and plucked fat grubs from the stalk, popping them into their mouths and chewing hungrily. They made their way into the dense forest near the river bank and peeled the bark back from a tree, scraping the fleshy part off with their teeth. Shoua had never cared for the fermented fish paste his family used to serve when they lived in the village, but even that was starting to sound tasty with his belly so empty.

When Shoua's cousins finally returned from their long journey into Thailand and back, they brought two types of flotation devices. One was a circular life ring which made it difficult to swim and nearly impossible to help pull another person- the user ends up spinning in the current, unable to exert much control over the ring's direction. The other was a thin inflatable that is blown up using a small tube. Because the latter is tied around the back and fits across the chest, the user can swim and pull other people to safety. The boys also tore their clothes into a makeshift rope around their waists so they wouldn't lose each other. The clothes were so old, however, they ripped easily once in the water. Shoua somehow remained tied to his cousin. Once fitted, Shoua dropped his carbine gun on the ground and made his way along the bank of the river. As they made their way into the water, the boys swallowed back their terror. Drowning is not considered an "accident" to the Hmong; it is because a dragon pulled the bather under. Because of this belief, shared by followers of shamanism and Christians alike, the Hmong avoided deep water. Entering the water of the mighty Mekong River without knowing how to swim was an act of courage and desperation.

Figure 1, Mekong River

Figure 2, Mekong River. The Mekong is a wide, murky river. Where it narrows the current is stronger and choppier. A boat can pass for miles in Laos without seeing a bridge span her waters, even today.
Photos (Figure 1 & 2) taken by author, Luang Prabang, Laos

It was the rainy season and the water was so full it took on a yellow tint and spilled onto the banks. Shoua thought the river looked like a vast ocean. With no moon, it was terrifying not being able to see. While this was a blessing—soldiers on watch on the banks couldn't see them as easily—it made navigating across the river that much more intimidating. Farther down, some fleeing men waded into the Mekong and hefted their machine guns over their heads to keep them dry during the crossing. The men felt better having their guns at the ready in order to protect their families from the border patrol–on either side–who may shoot. Once they made it to the Thai side of the river, their possessions (guns, canteens, money and flashlights) were confiscated by Thai police.

Those who didn't drown while trying to make the crossing often encountered Lao border guards patrolling along the shore or in gunboats. Refugees have shared harrowing stories of family members who were forced at gunpoint to get into the boats, only to be taken to the concentration camps back in Laos. Others witnessed loved ones struggling in the current, torrents of bullets ripping up the water all around them. Many did not live to bear witness at all.

Shoua and his cousins could just make out a streetlight through the trees, far downstream on the Thai side of the river. That light became the exit destination and beacon of hope for the boys. As they tried to navigate the current, they could only kick below the water, not splash or use their arms or they might be seen. They fought the strong current that continually tried to suck them back to the shores of Laos and prayed no boat patrol drifted by. Whirling in the powerful swells, they fought to direct their thin bodies towards the far shore, towards Thailand, towards safety.

Their muscles burning and teeth chattering, the boys were at the mercy of the river's current and they passed their landmark -the streetlamp- by quite a margin. When they were finally able to reach the shore of Thailand, they clawed their way up the steep embankment. Shoua cursed his luck. While there had been gentler landing sites, the river had chosen to deposit them here, with a wall of dirt and mud yet to climb. Exhausted, they hauled themselves up, digging small holes to create footing and grabbing roots and handfuls of earth to leverage them to the top. They eventually found steps Thai people had carved into the hill to get to their boats and the boys used those indentations the rest of the way. Once they cleared the top of the embankment, they rolled into the long grasses to catch their breath. The boys were wet, cold and clad only in their underwear.

The boys followed a well-worn path, rubbing their hands along their arms in an effort to create some warmth. The river had been cold, but it was the fear and anxiety of the unknown that was creating the chill they felt to their bones. The path led them to a village where the boys encountered locals who were used to seeing wet, hungry, scared refugees entering at all hours. Some villagers led the boys to a shelter where they would spend the night before being taken to a camp for processing. Shoua felt grateful that no one in the village had beaten them, as he had heard the stories of refugees who were "welcomed" into Thailand by being robbed and hit.

Shoua and his cousins were taken to a hut where they would spend the remainder of the evening. As someone pointed to the cement floor where they were to sleep, Shoua took in his surroundings. He had been offered no pillow, blankets or mattress and he possessed no extra clothing. Sleep eluded him as he tried to get comfortable on the hard surface. He reflected that even in the jungle where he had slept on the earth and leaves, there was some give, some small softness provided by the cushioning of the earth. Cement offered no such minor comfort. The hardness was especially profound due to his emaciated frame. Shoua simply had nothing on his thin body to provide any relief from the unyielding concrete. Shoua drew his bony knees to his chest and closed his eyes, wondering when he would be reunited with his mother and sisters, uncles and aunts. While he trusted his cousins, it would be reassuring to have adults around to help guide and protect him. He tried to distract himself from his hunger pangs by listening to the new sounds that greeted him. The crickets chirped a Thai welcome, the only creatures that seemed to offer him any acknowledgment on this dark night. It seemed to take forever before a troubled sleep finally overtook him.

In the morning, the six boys rose stiffly from their uncomfortable positions, rubbing their eyes. Today they would be processed for entry into the camp. Shoua wondered what the camp would be like, how long he would live there and what his life would be like afterwards. It was all so overwhelming- a lot for the boy to process. Shoua felt a tap on his shoulder. He spun around and eyed an eight-year-old girl who was holding something in her hand. She extended her arm, sharing whatever it was she held. Shoua accepted the small package quizzically. Who was this child and what was she offering? As she smiled at him and skipped away, Shoua's focus returned to the gift he held lightly in his palm. It was a banana leaf and inside was a small portion of sticky rice. In his hunger, he didn't remember having ever tasted anything more delicious. Over the next few mornings, the girl would appear with the rice for breakfast. Shoua suspected she was sent by her mother who must have taken pity on him. He never understood why the girl chose to help him, but his gratitude has endured for over forty years. He remembers the girl and her life-giving rice with fondness and vocalizes his desire to find her and thank her. "She saved my life", he recalls quietly.

Chapter 7
The In-Between: Life in the Refugee camps

The bus exited the main road and turned onto a dirt lane, kicking up swaths of dust. Shoua's small frame bounced from side to side as the bus rode over potholes in the road. The brakes squealed as the driver approached the gates to the camp. Shoua peered out of the grimy window and his heart sank at the sight of his new, temporary home. He saw brown everywhere–dirt paths, cement structures, more dirt. There were few trees in the area and the ones he saw looked thin and spindly. Perhaps most disturbing was the barbed wire fence encompassing the entire camp and the guards armed with side arms and machine guns who stood poised at the entrance. As the bus stopped inside the gates, Shoua exited, empty-handed. He owned no worldly possessions and brought only trepidation and hope with him to the camp.

As he leaped from the bottom step of the bus, Shoua's foot throbbed in pain. He was alarmed at how red and puffy it had become lately. Pointing to his foot, Shoua asked an elderly man where he could get help. The wrinkled hand pointed Shoua in the direction of the medical clinic run by the UN. He hobbled in the direction indicated and sat heavily in the chair as the doctor examined him. When Shoua had stepped in the elephant dung a good-sized sliver of wood had embedded itself in his foot which had become infected and swollen. The doctor informed young Shoua that if he had gone another two days with his foot in that condition he wouldn't have made it, his infection was so advanced.

At that time, Shoua was also treated with vitamins and medication to aid in digestion. He was so emaciated at this point that his body would struggle to digest the food that was being provided at the camp. His system was unused to having solid food and salt on a regular basis. Previous to his entrance in the refugee camp, Shoua recalls having gone months without salt. While this is difficult for westerners to conceptualize due to the abundance of processed foods which are high in salt, it is not something that is taken for granted by someone whose diet consists mostly of rice, vegetables and most recently of wild potatoes. The author of *Salt, a World History*, shares, "Salt deficiency causes headaches and weakness, then light-headedness, then nausea. If deprived long enough, the victim will die." Perhaps because of this need for the mineral, salt has been a valuable commodity for centuries. The revenue earned from salt and iron monopolies in China helped to fund the construction of the Great Wall. American aid to Laos around the time of Shoua's birth consisted largely of air drops of rice, ammunition, medical supplies–and salt. The book continues, "In Vietnam salt is so appreciated that poor people sometimes make a meal of nothing more than rice and a salt blend, either salt and chili powder or the more expensive salt with ground, grilled sesame seeds. Salt is also mixed with grilled ginger root." Because of the sudden introduction of salt back into his diet Shoua's skin would swell and when he pushed his finger down on his skin, it sank. The medication he was given caused him to have to get up to urinate throughout the night and, in Shoua's words, "get skinny. Eat, get puffy, pee all night". It took his body four to five months to be able to metabolize and process foods normally again.

The refugee camps in Thailand were run by several organizations, including the United Nations High Commission for Refugees (UNHCR), the International Organization for Migration (IOM), the International Rescue Committee, Refugees International and the Thai Ministry of the Interior. Shoua lived in several refugee camps over the next year and a half, including

Non Kai and Ban Vanai (Ban is the Thai word for village), a 400 acre camp built in 1975. By 1985, there were 50,000 people living in a camp originally built for 12,000 Hmong soldiers and their families. The camp was eventually closed in 1995 as Thailand's initial welcome of the refugees had worn thin.

Life in a refugee camp is squalid. In addition to the over-crowded living conditions, people who live there describe having enough food to eat only three days of the week. The open sewage canals create a stink that lingers in people's memories. Food and medical supplies are scarce, toilet facilities woefully inadequate, diseases run rampant, and hunger is common. Food drops only occur a few days a week, so families struggle to feed their children with rice and whatever vegetables they can grow in the tiny plots of inhospitable soil near the shelters. While relief agencies occasionally provided meat, it is often rotten. Shoua recalled receiving tins of water buffalo meat supplied by the refugee groups. The family warmed the meat on their wood stove and spread the portions thinly to feed the large family living in the shelter. Cheap—not necessarily fresh- fruit and vegetables were distributed and, according to Jane Hamilton-Merritt, "the rice was broken and contained stones and rat droppings, indicating it was probably floor sweepings from rice mills, fit only for animal feed". Shoua and his cousin's family chewed their rice carefully as it contained sand, which was very unpleasant. He had assumed the sand made its way into the rice bags when the bags were dropped off the back of the truck onto the dusty road until he heard rumors that the people paid to fill the bags added the sand intentionally so the bags weighed more and they made more money. As the war progressed, thousands of Hmong sought refuge in the camps. Since many were there unofficially and therefore considered to be there illegally, they had no food rations at all. Although he was in the camp legally, Shoua still struggled to get enough to eat. And yet it was safer here than returning to Laos, where the Hmong faced imprisonment, torture or death.

Refugee camps have been called a "breeding ground for disease" as outbreaks of cholera, malaria, hepatitis, and para-sitic diseases run rampant where there are so many people in a confined space. Malnourishment is a chronic condition in the camps and makes the refugees–especially children–more susceptible to contracting disease. Many illnesses cause diarrhea, leading to severe dehydration which is difficult to treat in areas where water is a limited commodity. Jaundice is often seen in areas where living conditions are overcrowded and unsanitary and makes the sufferer more susceptible to disease. If a refugee was fortunate enough to be in good health upon arrival at the camps, they may find it challenging to remain healthy for long.

The bathroom consisted of a cement tank that was emptied once a week. It was unclean and filled with flies and the stench was made unbearable due to the moist, clinging air. Because the sewage tanks were rarely emptied, people were forced to evacuate their bowels wherever they could find space. The stink was overwhelming and there were flies everywhere, even clinging to freshly drying laundry on the lines. Since the streets were not paved, vehicles splattered dirt and red mud on everything in their path, leaving grit that seemed to cover every surface.

Tens of thousands of people occupied a small geographical space and in some camps families with as many as twelve or more people shared a space originally built for two airmen. Since water was only available from a tank twice a day, camp inhabitants learned that if they dug deep enough, they would encounter the water table. They would lower a bucket–by hand–into the hole and haul up the muddy water. It was drinkable after it sat for a while and the debris settled to the bottom. It was under these conditions that refugees lived for years, and in some cases decades, as they waited for the opportunity to be transferred to a permanent host country.

There is an expression in Southeast Asia, "Same, Same–but Different". The various refugee camps were like this. Each camp felt like a waiting room, a warehouse of human suffering as families killed time until their real lives, their new lives in a safer country, could begin. Yet each camp possessed its own unique flavor as well- different smells, colors, nuances of landscape and terrain. Shoua remembers one of the camps as having rocky ground, so when the rains came the walking wasn't too difficult. The rocks provided relatively firm footing, a place to place your feet when the soggy earth was slippery. Another camp, however, turned into a sticky, thick red mud during the rains, the kind that sucks the shoes right off your feet if you were fortunate enough to own shoes.

Refugees from other camps have described murders, rapes and beatings and no consequences for the perpetrators of these terrifying crimes. One man from an African refugee camp shared that the translator assigned to help the displaced people stole his documentation and paperwork. As a result, the refugees couldn't leave and ended up living in the camp for nearly twenty years. People are in these camps due to the horrors they faced during their displacement from their communities. It is incredulous to think that they are further victimized in the very place that is meant to be a temporary haven.

In Shoua's camp at Non-Khai, housing was cramped, to say the least. Units consisted of long cement bunkers divided into 15 units on each side, or thirty rooms per building. Each family lived in one room often cramming eight, ten, twelve or more children in with parents, grandparents, aunts and uncles. There was no privacy. All of the sounds and smells mingled together, the press of humanity felt keenly in such a confined space. Cooking was done in a grass house located just outside of the bunkers. This is where Shoua slept. His younger cousin slept there as well but did not often come home before midnight, so Shoua had the small space to himself most evenings.

Figure 1,   Ban Vinai Refugee camp in Thailand. Shoua lived in the building on the top row, second structure in.
Photo courtesy of Shoua Her

Shoua rose early and stretched his limbs. He rolled up his thin woven mat and tipped the bamboo frame on its side, leaning it against the wall of the grass hut. He enjoyed this time of day. It was a little cooler, so the stench of the camp wasn't so overpowering. Most of the people in the camp were still asleep and he enjoyed the quiet, the birdsong and the delicious feeling of stealing a few minutes for himself. The peacefulness didn't last. Soon the family was stirring, and Shoua was busy hauling water in aluminum buckets from the hand drawn well and lighting the fire. He leaned over the iron pot and examined the supply of tightly pressed wood chips they used as fuel in their makeshift bamboo grill. The wood chips were running low. He made a mental note to arrange for a pass in order to take the hour-long taxi ride south to buy more. The manager of each of the thirty housing units handed out six passes a day for refugees to leave the compound. The six passes were good for the entire day, so if one person ran into the city to sign documents and were back within a few hours they would simply hand the pass over to someone else to use. Shoua would need 500 Thai baht, or the equivalent of $2 in late 1970s exchange rates for the taxi ride and wood chips. Doing repairs using bamboo was simpler. Shoua would just sneak out of the camp and gather what he needed from the clusters surrounding the camp.

As he prepared the fire to cook the family's breakfast, Shoua listened to the echo of the shaman's drum beats, guiding the souls of the recently departed to their ancestral homeland. The sound of the drums and the accompanying wailing of grief-stricken family members sent chills down his spine. The drums beat day and night throughout the camp, a constant reminder of the fragility of life and the inescapable reality of death in this hostile environment. As he walked across the compound to buy supplies, Shoua lowered his eyes to avoid looking at the wall.

The dead body had been lying on the bamboo mat for almost a week, and the smell of rot was thick in the air. (In the villages, bodies were left in state for up to twelve days in order to allow enough time for distant relatives to come and pay their respect. The tradition continued in the camps.) The body lay on a plank and was raised against the wall, so the body laid flat but was waist high to a passerby; much like a window washer's platform is hoisted up the side of a building. Whoever lay on the boards had been carefully dressed by their family in the official garb of the dead, including slippers made of hemp. The slippers were to be used to cross one of several mountains for judgment in the afterlife. Female relatives bent over the body, fanning away flies. The beat of the funeral drums, made from a hollowed tree trunk and covered with cowhide, reverberated against the wall. Haunting music came from the *qeej*, the reeded bamboo instrument played at funerals. The man playing the *qeej* changed the direction of his footwork often as he walked to "confuse any spirits trying to follow him in order to bring sickness or death into the world of the living." The haunting music they created "links the physical world with the spiritual realm, creating safe passage as the deceased's soul reaches the ancestral homeland". Mourners nearby covered their faces with white cloth so the dead wouldn't recognize them and take their souls.

Figure 2,   Men playing the qeej. The instrument is never played in the house. Men often learn to play and practice their music in the forest to minimize any consequences incurred by stirring up evil spirits. Photo from the Lao National Museum in Vientiane, Laos, used by permission.

The dead person's soul must make a long journey to return to their ancestral homeland. This travel–with the help of a shaman–takes the soul back through every place they had lived in order to return to the place where their parents had buried the placenta of the deceased. When a daughter is born, her placenta is buried under her parent's bed. The placenta of a son is buried in the place of honor, underneath the central post of the thatched house. The soul can then retrieve its placental jacket–the word for placenta in Hmong means "one's first jacket" –and begin its journey to the sky. In order to return, however, the soul must make the journey back. This became very arduous for families when they moved to the United States and lost loved ones, as the journey became longer and more complicated than it had been in the high mountains of Laos. For example, if a Hmong person originally from Laos died in California but had first lived in Minnesota, the soul would need to board the plane in California, make it to Minnesota, board the plane to Thailand to go back to each of the camps in which they lived, return to the places he or she lived in the jungle before finally returning to the village home, eventually to be born again. All of this is done via the shaman who works under a trance and guides the soul through the process. The family burns token money made of rice paper so the deceased can (symbolically) pay for travel expenses such as airplane tickets and bridge crossing fees and money to pay necessary bribes during their spirit journey. The family places a boiled chicken in the casket under the head of the deceased to provide food during the journey. In the United States, Hmong families utilize mortuary services, but in the camps they followed traditional burial practices. The body on the wall would be removed after about a week before being carried to an open field. There, the body was allowed to sit out all afternoon before finally being buried. A man fired an arrow from a crossbow over the grave to ward away evil spirits. Shoua noticed a body that had been recently buried in an auspicious place, next to the trail. He concluded the dead person must have been an elder to have been buried in such a place of honor. The shaman and mourners would place a bamboo pole with the leaves still attached in the middle of the burial site and throw clothes on top. The family eats and sits together for up to a week during the elaborate funeral procedures.

Shoua glanced at the field as he passed by and noticed the bamboo leaves and clothes fluttering in the breeze. He shuddered at the image. He heard the rattle of the divining horns as the shaman threw them down, like dice. Shamans will sometimes use divining tools made of cow or water buffalo horns cut in half, lengthwise. Used to communicate with the spirit world, the divination horns were tossed while asking a question about "the cause of an illness, accident or misfortune". If the horn pieces landed parallel and flat side up, the answer was that ancestor spirits caused the problem. Rounded sides up and parallel and the ancestor spirits want offerings of food in the form of a cow or chicken. Rounded sides up but crossed meant the "spirits have taken an ill person who will not survive". Rounded sides up and at a 90-degree angle to each other were interpreted to mean "the subject is in serious condition and will die. When the family buries the deceased, the family must sacrifice a chicken." Finally, one rounded side up and one flat side up means "a spirit is the cause of the problem, and the shaman must ask what it wants in place of the ill or hurt person."

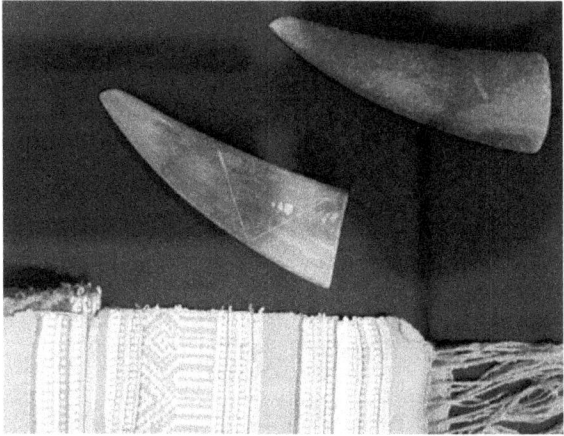

Figure 3, Divining tools are made from cow or water buffalo horns. Photo taken by the author and used with permission of The Traditional Arts and Ethnology Centre (TAEC) in Luang Prabang, Laos

Shamanism is a central component in the lives of two-thirds of Hmong people. A shaman can bridge the physical and spiritual worlds and is called upon by the spirits to practice healing. He (or sometimes she) often gets his power while struggling with an illness himself. It is during that time of personal illness that the future healer is tapped by the spirit world. That individual then becomes a shaman and is able to connect ill Hmong community members and the spirit world for the purposes of healing. Shamanism is a mixture of medical and spiritual practice that helps to heal the physical body or bring back its wandering soul through communicating with spirits or ancestors from the other world. Hmong who practice shamanism believe the body contains more than one soul, possibly as many as seven, and they guard against one or more of the souls wandering off. They also believe in animism, or the idea that non-human beings and objects have souls. This is the reason that cows, pigs and chickens are sacrificed when a person is sick, as the soul of the animal is being bartered for the soul of the sick individual, whose soul may have wandered. Sometimes the sacrifice is made to "confuse the passage of the evil spirits to this world, as a kind of decoy."

Dr. Robert Cooper explains in his book, *The Hmong, a Traditional Life*: "Full mortuary rites are not performed for everyone. The souls of those killed mysteriously or violently are thought to assume the shape of hungry ghosts, and their bodies are disposed of as quickly as possible, with the barest of preliminaries. If there is a funeral for them, their bodies may not be carried out of the house through the door; a special opening must be made in the side of the house. The same is done with the bodies of stillborn children, or those who die within the first three days of life. Such children lack souls since they have not undergone the appropriate soul-calling and naming rituals and funeral rites cannot be performed for them... The family of the deceased are usually very keen to pay off all debts of their relatives since debts outstanding in this life will be carried over into the next, and in popular belief may result in rebirth as a pig or other animal in the household of the debtor."

While funerals are the most elaborate ceremonies conducted by the Hmong, shamanism pervades many of the lesser challenges and milestones in life as well. When one of the family's chickens suffered a broken leg, Shoua recounts that an elder put medicine on the leg of the table in the home. The herbs, carefully tied to the wooden table leg, supposedly healed the chicken.

Traditional Hmong had other beliefs that border on the fantastic. During a lunar eclipse, it was reasoned that the devil had eaten the moon, so men fired gunshots in an effort to protect the moon. When a person dies, three shots are fired into the air to frighten away evil spirits "who may seek to attack the departing soul or his household". If a person's ears hurt, whether from the cold mountain air or from infection, it was believed the moon was responsible for cutting the ear. Men hunting in the mountains feared a devil that ate human flesh. In the evenings, when they were roasting squirrel or a bird over the fire for supper, the spirit was attracted to the scent and came after the humans. When the sun had settled behind the hills and darkness closed in, the men noticed a strange wind stirring the leaves. They heard the sounds of wild boar and monkeys, creatures that were usually silent after dusk. Knowing the spirits could transform into people, the men burned incense to keep evil away. The frightened men prayed for lightning to strike somewhere nearby to get rid of the evil–once it struck they knew they were safe.

Another tale of magical thinking involved one of Shoua's cousins who had relocated to Kansas, where he continued the traditional Hmong occupation of slash and burn farming. A second cousin moved to town and asked if he could farm the land next door; his cousin agreed. The new cousin cut down the trees to plant rice, leaving some trees standing to act as a natural border between the farms. The first cousin accused him of cheating him out of ten yards of his original property; the new cousin denied it. "You have cheated me!" the cousin cried, throwing his hoe to the ground in anger. The other cousin, his face red, shook his fist in rage at the accusation. This went on, each cousin shouting, glaring, and threatening the other until suddenly, lightning flashed from the sky, scorching the land and creating a natural border between the two pieces of property. It is said by the family that Shoua's cousin has never tried to cheat anyone since.

One afternoon Shoua stood waiting in line for his ration of food where he observed a baby strapped to the back of the woman in line in front of him. He was careful not to tell the mother that her child was cute. In Hmong culture, people wouldn't tell a parent, "Your son is so handsome! Your daughter is beautiful!" Rather, they would say, "Your child is so ugly! He is so dirty!" so the evil spirits won't take the child's soul away. The child in line was wearing white cords around his wrists which shamans had blessed to protect him and keep his souls inside of his body. The colorful hat worn by the baby had a maze design woken into it, designed to keep the baby close to its mother and to keep its soul from wandering. In these ways, Hmong parents did all they could to keep their children safe from harm.

In addition to sewing beautiful designs on baby clothes, many Hmong women would create story clothes using embroidery, batik, applique and reverse applique in the refugee camps to sell to relief workers, missionaries or to send to relatives to sell overseas. Embroidery is an important craft for Hmong women. As with so many cultural arts, it is lost on newer generations and there is a movement to keep the practice alive. Traditionally, the skill was passed from mother to daughter and the embroidery depicted scenes from farming, village life and nature (later story clothes included scenes from the war). It was mostly used for new clothes in New Year's celebrations and is called *paj ntaub* (pronounced pawn-dough, sometimes spelled in the westernized version, pandau), or "flower cloth" in Hmong. According to an article in *The Star Tribune*, "In ancient times, the embroidered patterns served double duty- to decorate and to communicate. According to oral history, long ago when the Hmong were still concentrated in China, they were forbidden to use their original, written language, which was made up of picture symbols. So, the women started sewing the symbols into their skirts to create messages, disguising them as patterns... Today, no one can decode those messages, because the original language's meaning has been lost". The story clothes capture important scenes, symbolism, and memories. Women often sew intricate symbols into the panel cloth, including tiger paw prints, which represent a spirit animal passing by. Many Hmong believe that tigers can take over a person's spirit. If the soul of the spirit tiger turns evil, it becomes a magic soul-tiger and the embroidery will reflect that by showing a five toed tiger print instead of the normal four toes. Other symbols include snail shells which represent family growth and interconnectedness, as well as centipedes, which are highly respected for their medicinal qualities. *Paj ntaub* are art.

Figure 4, Typical scene from Hmong paj ntaub
Photo taken by the author, permission of the Asian Pacific
Development Center, Aurora, Colorado

Figure 5, Story cloth went from depicting village life, animals and
geographic designs to also incorporating the horrors of war.
Photo taken by the author, permission of the Asian Pacific
Development Center, Aurora, Colorado

The sister-in-law of the family with whom Shoua stayed in the camp created *paj ntaub* to sell for income for the family. Because of her preoccupation with embroidery, the cooking and cleaning was left to Shoua. He did his best to please his host family so they would continue to allow him to live with them. Orphaned, he relied on the generosity of his uncle, his uncle's son (who had been wounded in combat) and even his own nephew. So young Shoua cooked and cleaned to ensure his continued housing and survival. He was grateful for the shelter and protection his extended family offered him, but he missed his own family terribly. Shoua found his thoughts drawn again and again to his mother, sister and little niece. He worried over their safety and wondered how they would make it to the camp. Were they finding enough food to eat? Was the little girl staying quiet? He felt the anxious unknown in the pit of his stomach, a talisman of longing, hope and fear.

Figure 6, This is the cousin's family where Shoua lived while at Non-Khai camp in Thailand. Shoua is in the back row, second from the left. He is standing on a rise and appears almost as tall as his cousin on the left.
Photo courtesy of Shoua Her

Shoua's cousin told him about a person who had left their camp to look for lost family members. The cousin said the person was able to bring people to the processing center in Thailand and then sneak back into the camp. Shoua found himself consumed with worry and hope for his remaining family. Had his mother, sister and niece made it to safety with this brave soul? Shoua made discreet enquiries until he discovered the man who had broken out of the camp and then back in again. Shoua approached him and stated, "I heard you brought some families into Thailand!"

"Yes- we got lucky. The rain was horrible so there were no gunboats on the river last night. They were all pretty tired, but they made it. I left them at the processing center–They should be at the other camp soon."

"Do you know Chue and her little girl, Bao?" (Shoua's sister and niece) he asked.

"Yes! They were there, they made it."

"And Mai?" (Shoua's Mom)

"No- she passed away. Someone went to check on her and found her leaning against a bamboo thicket. When they called her, she didn't respond–she had already died. I'm sorry. They did find her ID and a picture of her with her husband, though," he offered quietly. Shoua later recovered that picture from his sister and still has the photo to this day. Shoua had now lost both of his parents to starvation.

When his father had died, Shoua had been distracted from his feelings because of his encounter with the tiger and his pressing need to catch up with his family. Now he was surrounded by what remained of his family and there were no tigers to distract him. He found himself orphaned and under the care of his aunts, uncles, and cousins. Without his mother and father there to protect and guide him, Shoua suddenly felt as if he had lost his sense of direction. Even when he hadn't physically been with his parents, knowing they were out there had fortified him somehow. Now that they were both gone, he felt like a boat without a rudder, a starry sky with no known constellations. He felt lost. Shoua wondered if this meant he must now be a man.

Shoua was saddened that he and his family were not able to give his mother or father a proper burial, although he took comfort in his Christian beliefs that they were in heaven. If he had practiced shamanism, he would have worried that their souls would not be able to find their way back to their place of birth, an important step in the death process of the Hmong. Shoua would have insisted on a ceremony to release the souls of the dead so that they might be reborn. With no shaman to guide their spirits, their souls may be left to wander. As it was, Shoua was the one left to wander.

Shoua tried to keep busy to distract himself from his grief. Attending English classes provided that opportunity. Some education was provided in the camps for children, but they were mostly taught in the Thai language. Shoua had no interest in learning to speak or read Thai as he felt strongly, "This is not my place. Thailand is not my home". He knew the camps in Thailand were a temporary living arrangement–temporary by months or years, he did not know–and he did not feel a connection or loyalty to the country. He did take advantage of the classes held in the evenings that taught refugees how to write Basic English, especially how to sign their names in English. This would be very important as they applied for exile in the United States and would be required to sign official documents and applications. After 1980, the evening schools would teach other "western" skills such as how to dial a phone, turn on a stove and work a light switch. While these sound like very basic concepts, they were completely foreign to a people whose every basic need had been met by the jungle. In later years, the camp also began providing refugees with plastic shoes to wear. When Shoua lived there, however, this was not a luxury he enjoyed. He had to make do with any money his brother Vang and his cousins could afford to send him. Vang had sent Shoua the equivalent of $100 in Thai Bhat currency. Shoua used this money to purchase shoes and clothes from the small store that sold supplies to the refugees at inflated prices. He saved the remaining money for his journey to America. He would eventually enter the United States with 20 American dollars to his name.

Chapter 8
The Interview

To be granted entry to the United States, Shoua and the other refugees were required to go through a multi-step interview process with immigration officials to determine their eligibility. When Shoua's interview date was at hand, he arrived at 7:00 am, as instructed. He observed his surroundings, noting the corrugated steel roof, the press of people waiting to be called, and the sense of anticipation and anxiety in the air. Shoua wondered how long he would have to wait and what questions they would ask him. What if he didn't know the answers? He sat back and tried to find a comfortable position in which to wait.

Asylum is requested based on past persecution or fear of future persecution if the refugee is forced to return to their homeland. It is the difficult job of the interviewer to determine who is lying and using the system to get to a new homeland and who is in genuine need of emergency relocation. Refugees are asked a series of questions by an interviewer, then asked the same questions months later to see if the answers are consistent. This is done to ascertain that the person is who they say they are and that the refugee will be an asset to the host country, not a liability. Immigration officers also have an opportunity to do fact checking and corroborating stories between interviews as they want to ensure that a non-deserving person isn't qualifying for relocation. Questions asked of the Hmong during this time period included the number of siblings a person has, when and how they arrived in the camp, what battles they were involved in, and in what capacity. If the refugee answers the questions the same way in the second interview held six or so months later, then the likelihood increases that the individual is who they claim to be. People's petitions for asylum have been declined as a result of failing their interviews; some men gave the wrong information about battles they claimed to have been involved in and they were therefore denied entry to the US. Officers are on alert for the interviewee whose story is airtight, extremely logical and well-rehearsed. They noticed those whose emotional affect was very limited as most people who have experienced the horrors requiring refugee status will display a break in their narrative as they share their painful stories.

Immigration officials have reported that some of their interviewees have a significant startle response, meaning they noticeably jump at noises for which most people would only turn their heads. Some applicants are torture survivors and demonstrate this type of hypervigilance, caused by trauma. While being held captive, they would hear the cells next to them clanging open and shut as their persecutors collected fellow prisoners to be beaten. If a loud noise erupts near them, these survivors might seem to jump out of their skin in response.

The Refugee Act of 1980 was passed in an effort to provide more structured and uniform procedures to help in resettlement efforts. The act made provisions for developing budgets, resettlement programs, grants and partnerships with volunteer agencies. When Shoua was being processed, however, things were being done in a more ad hoc manner. Officers weren't as aware of the effects of torture and war on refugees, and sometimes mistook their jumbled chronologies as deceptiveness and intentional falsehoods. It would be years before trainings would inform interviewers of the effects of severe trauma on mental processing. Later challenges to the system would include increased bureaucracy including an emphasis on providing proof of documentation, a near impossibility for most people fleeing prosecution. It is very difficult for a person applying for group protection (for example, Christians being slaughtered due to their religion) to provide evidence that they were personally threatened. Nevertheless, officers and the system in which they work continue to evolve, striving to provide refuge and protection to those whose lives depend on it and screen out the rest.

This same process was used with Chinese immigrants on the so-called "Ellis Island of the West", an immigration station on Angel Island within viewing distance of San Francisco. Immigrants were asked questions by interrogators and then asked again at a later date to check for veracity. In this way, officials hoped to separate those who were legitimately joining family members from those who had created a "paper father" or "paper son"–a false familial relationship–in order to gain access to citizenship. Sometimes the questions being asked were obscure enough to confuse even the most forthright individual, such as, "How many windows are in your house?" In the case of Angel Island, immigrant hopefuls were not allowed to leave. The bunkers became their prison for months and in some cases years before being admitted into the Unites States or being sent back to China. In the refugee camp in Thailand, people simply had no place else to go.

Before making his way to the United States, Vang talked quietly with his cousin and his cousin's wife in the refugee camp. He explained to them that his parents were back in Laos and he didn't think they would ever get out (Vang relocated before Shoua, so to the best of Vang's knowledge, his parents were still alive at this time). Vang knew he was well qualified to be accepted in the United States as he had worked with the CIA and at that time the US was only accepting applicants who had served the US military in some capacity. Since the cousin had not fought with the US military, Vang asked him and his wife to pretend to be his parents and in return Vang would take their older son to America, as Vang's "brother". In this way, Vang lied to his interviewer in order to carve a path for himself to America. The cousin later felt guilty about his lie, as it would have been discovered during the interview with subsequent family members when the officer tried to corroborate his story. Realizing that other relatives would be denied entry into the US because of his fabrication, the cousin recanted his story. This caused the cousin to fail his interview and ruined his chances of being admitted to the US as a refugee (Vang had already made it to the US at this point). The cousin spent the next seven years living in the camps until the camps were eventually closed and all refugees were either relocated to the US or sent back to Laos (Shoua's cousin was finally sent to the US). Vang was eventually able to bring his sister and his older brother's wife, both widowed during the war, and their children to the United States. While he was in the camps, the cousin communicated with Shoua via letters and cassette tapes. They would record conversations and questions to each other via the tapes, as cell phones were years into the future. That meager connection to family, however tenuous, was very powerful for both of the Her males.

Shoua sat, waiting for his "T" number to be called. The number was a case identifier, likely a precursor to the "A" number immigrants and refugees would be assigned to in later years. Questioning took place in a large room covered by an aluminum roof which did nothing to mitigate the heat of the humid, 90-degree day. In this oven-like environment, Shoua tried to fan himself which also kept the flies at bay for a few precious seconds until they settled on his skin yet again. While he knew he needed to remain in the building until his number was called, Shoua would at times escape the stifling heat and venture outdoors where there was no tin roof to suppress a breeze. This was made easier during the time of year when the rice had been harvested as it made walking through rice paddies easier. This was a risk, though. If his number was called and Shoua wasn't present, he would have to wait three months for the next opportunity for an interview. Shoua snuck outside several times throughout the day, fervently hoping his number wouldn't be called while he gulped air a few degrees cooler than the interrogation building. Bored from the tedium of waiting, he plucked a blade of grass, held it between his thumbs and held it to his lips. The sound he created amused him for a few minutes until he made his way back into the stifling building with the corrugated roof.

After a drink from the water tank that applicants could visit twice a day and after several hours of waiting to hear his number called, Shoua needed to find a toilet. It was in this environment that 13-year-old Shoua waited. He had arrived on his interrogation day at 7:00 am, as expected. He was not called for questioning until 4:00pm. He sat listening to the loudspeakers of the camp calling people to the clinic for their medical checks and others to the field where they would board a bus for Bangkok. He played with small pebbles by his feet and nervously wondered what these men would ask him. Would they be patient? Kind? Stern? Would he eventually hear his name called over that loudspeaker to be called to a bus transport or would he spend the rest of his life surrounded by a barbed wire fence, as his cousin would? Shoua wished for the tenth time that day that his parents were with him. He swatted at the flies, waiting.

When his number was finally called, Shoua made his way to the room where he had seen people entering and exiting all day. With butterflies in his stomach, he opened the door and sat down on the chair indicated, looking at the papers strewn on the scratched desk of the official. A white man sat at the table, wearing short sleeves due to the heat. The man rifled through some papers while eating a bowl of ice cream. Shoua, who had been living off old, cheap rice and canned meat, could only look at the icy treat in wonder. The man cleared his throat, shuffled his papers and began his questioning through an interpreter who spoke Hmong. Shoua tried to focus on answering clearly and honestly. He felt nervous, knowing his future and freedom were at stake. The man inquired how had Shoua gotten to the camp and what had his life been like before arrival. Did he have any family with him in the camps so they might join him when he left? Shoua struggled with how to answer this one. Two-thirds of Shoua's sisters had lost their husbands in the war and were now widows. He decided to tell the interrogator about the sister and her son living at the same camp. The official asked Shoua to go find her so she could apply for entry to the US with him. Shoua stood up quickly and ran to find his sister. On the way, he ran into his cousin and asked him if he thought Shoua should also tell the interrogator about his other sister and his little niece- the ones he had to leave behind who were now in Ban Vinai, the other major refugee camp. The cousin shook his head. "No- they'll hold you here for another year! I heard they make people wait until everyone is in the same camp before you can all leave. You'll be stuck here longer, Shoua." Shoua sadly thanked the cousin, found the sister who lived in the same camp and led her to the white man in the office. In this way, Shoua was able to bring some of his family with him on the journey to the United States.

Later, he chided himself about his decision. Had he done the right thing? Should he have told the man about his other sister? Maybe she could get out with him! But if his cousin was right, it would mean Shoua would be stuck in this stinking mud pit for another year, a thought he could not tolerate.

When Shoua passed his second round of questioning, it was determined that he was a legitimate candidate for refugee status in the United States. He was subjected to a medical check to ensure he would bring no disease to the US, specifically leprosy, tuberculosis, syphilis and other sexually contracted diseases or significant mental health conditions. After his initial acceptance, Shoua waited in the sweltering camp for another 3 months while his case was being processed. He then met with a panel of professionals; one took his fingerprints, another took his picture for his new documents and the third was a judge. The judge gave young Shoua a lecture, reminding him to not steal, to be a productive member of US society and to not commit any crimes in his new country. Shoua agreed to the conditions set forth and then waited another few months for his "T" number to be called. When it finally was, he was sent by bus to Bangkok, Thailand where he submitted to another physical exam at the hospital. After waiting four days for the results to prove his health, he was taken to the international airport in Bangkok where he signed forms and legal documents and waited all day and well into the evening for a flight to the US. After many months of waiting, hoping, enduring the heat, stench, and overcrowding, Shoua was finally able to leave Southeast Asia for his new home in America.

Figure 1, Non-Khai Refugee Camp. These are the buses refugees took to be relocated.
Photo courtesy of Shoua Her

Chapter 9
Transitions

The refugee facilities in Thailand marked the beginning of the end of family structure as most Hmong had known it up to that point. Camp life and subsequent life in America created a radical shift in the landscape of the Hmong family unit. There were sudden changes in traditional roles that created long-term effects on Hmong values, parenting, and dynamics between the genders and among generations.

Men were the providers and heads of household in traditional Hmong culture. This shifted drastically when they lived in the camps. While some men, including Shoua's cousin, were able to eek out a living by creating the silver necklaces so coveted by Hmong women, many found themselves with little to do in the camps. Men could no longer work in the fields or provide meaningful income for their families and instead found themselves in the unlikely position of relying on their wives for 90% of the family's income. By contrast, it was the women who were able to bring in money making their embroidery. Women for the first time were able to contribute to the family's revenue by selling their beautiful *paj ntaub* and that shifted the family power dynamic. This became more evident once families were living in America, when many younger Hmong women fought to become educated and have a more equal role in their marriages. Hmong women in the United States observed the freedom and relative equality enjoyed by American women and began to demand a shift in the way they participated in their relationships as wives, daughters, and mothers.

Some children attended school while in the camps but others, especially the boys, found themselves less accountable to the family than they had once been and roamed the camps, making mischief. This was a precursor to the gangs that would plague the resettled Hmong community in America. Girls were less likely to roam freely, as families kept a tight rein on their daughters to ensure their virtue before marriage. Most Hmong girls marry young, often at age 14, and some are involved with the cultural practice of "kidnap marriages", whereby a boy keeps a girl at his home for up to three days as his family's negotiators seek the approval of the bride's family and arrange a bride price. It is difficult for the girl's family to decline this marriage since much can happen in three days that could sully the girl's reputation and make her less desirable for another suitor. Sometimes these "kidnappings" are mutual; the young girl likes the boy and agrees to go to his house. Other times the girl knows she doesn't have a say in who she will marry, so she merely acquiesces. Some girls have completed suicide as a result of the forced match. Many Hmong still marry young in America, but more girls are delaying marriage and family in pursuit of education and a career.

Male elders of the village were the decision makers and enjoyed great respect in Hmong culture. Female elders were surrounded by their children (and in some cases the children of their husband's other wives) and grandchildren, sources of tremendous love and joy. In the camps, elders now found themselves faced with the daunting choice of either remaining in the camps with some of their children and grandchildren in Thailand or relocating to America (or another country) with their other children. Relocating entailed traveling around the world to a country where they did not speak the language or understand the culture. The older generation had very little hope of acculturation within their lifetime which meant they would spend the rest of their years completely dependent upon their children and grandchildren, an uncomfortable position for a revered elder. Some parents asked their children to shop at the store because they could not read what the boxes contained. Older Hmong immigrants recall their inability to cross the street in America without assistance, as there is no such thing as a crosswalk or traffic in the jungle villages. Other elders would never master the skill of using a telephone, so they were reliant upon the patience of their family to remain connected with others. Refugees from other countries have remarked upon similar challenges as they try to navigate the cultural nuances in their new homeland. In some countries in the Middle East, for example, there are no speed limits, red lights are considered optional if no other drivers are around and stop signs are seen as decorations. One can imagine the upset caused when the individual resettles in an American city that automatically issues tickets based on violations caught on camera at intersections.

Another challenge for some Hmong trying to resettle in the United States is a unique cultural practice. While polygamy is not practiced by all Hmong, it is sometimes practiced in Laos. Having multiple wives served several purposes. It added to the family's wealth, as more wives meant more time tending crops and therefore having more food and income. Some men had second and third wives as a result of so many men being killed in the war; marriage helped ensure the survival of the vulnerable women and children who were left on their own when the men in the family were killed. To be eligible for relocation, some men with multiple wives took the culturally drastic step of divorcing all but one. Some, such as Shoua's uncle, brought his wives over under the guise of various roles. One was his "wife", one was his "sister", and another was his "cousin". In this way, he was able to keep his family intact. Other men chose to stay in the camps indefinitely, as they were not eligible for relocation unless they divorced one or more of their wives. Divorce is taboo in traditional Hmong culture although it is becoming more commonplace in current times with younger generations born and raised in the United States. These men did not want to leave any of their wives behind and felt morally obligated to care for them. Children go with the father or the father's family if there is a divide in a marriage, so the men would have not only left their wives, but left those women childless as well. The culture shock must be enormous to go from a country where it is beneficial – even noble – to take on additional wives to one where it is illegal and considered immoral. Nonetheless, families adapted to the changes in their structural unit to accommodate the expectations of their new homeland.

One refugee to the United States shared her experience at an immigration health clinic. The clinic staff members were inquiring about the health of each applicant, including teenagers and children. The woman was shocked and appalled when the immigration clinician asked her young teenage daughter if she was sexually active. "That is simply not something you would ask in my country!" the woman explained. *Of course,* her daughter was a virgin, and would remain so until marriage! It was culturally inappropriate, in her opinion, for the health worker to have asked such a question, much less to have directed the question at the teenager. The family was deeply offended and told their daughter not to answer. Such are the cultural nuances one encounters when east meets west and when traditional parenting meets more liberal parenting.

Hmong families changed their names from clan name first to given name first, as is traditional in western cultures. Shoua, for example, would have been known by "Her", his clan name, first and his given name, Shoua, second. Thus, the very identities of refugees changed including everything from traditional roles and values to how they were introduced.

People such as Shoua flee their homeland with few possessions to avoid being exterminated by a pursuing enemy. The implications of being an immigrant vs. a refugee are enormous. Immigration is a planned event. The family has time to make decisions about their home and business, to say goodbye to loved ones and to sell valuables and pack the treasures they want to bring with them to the new homeland. In short, immigration is a choice (unless it is a forced immigration, as was the case with African slaves) even though that choice may be influenced by very challenging and stressful motivators such as escaping crushing poverty or freedom from religious persecution. Refugees are fleeing for their lives. A person may be displaced due to environmental factors such as a devastating hurricane or earthquake or become a refugee for political reasons- perhaps a new dictator has placed a price on someone's head due to their beliefs or connections. One refugee from Africa escaped to a camp because he had a death sentence due to his parents' biracial marriage. People also become refugees in response to genocide, as we have seen in Poland and Germany in World War Two, and and later decades in Rwanda, Bosnia, Myanmar, and with the Hmong. Refugees are more susceptible to other stressors such as "culture shock, homesickness, depression, distress, stress-related illnesses, posttraumatic stress disorder, exit and post entry trauma and acculturation stress." In short, refugees face all of these issues in addition to the horrors that caused them to flee in the first place, compounding their stress. This is not insurmountable, however, as Shoua and so many others have demonstrated.

There is also a distinct difference in social stratification as to which *wave* a person arrived in the United States, especially after the Vietnam War. Early waves of Vietnamese immigrants consisted of educated professionals who were able to bring their accumulated wealth and often had contacts, families or sponsors in their new homelands. Vietnamese families from later waves arrived in overcrowded boats instead of passenger ships and were referred to as "boat people". The boats were often overtaken by pirates who robbed families of their valuables and raped nearly all of the women aboard. These refugees brought little with them and were forced to rely on the generosity of their new country more than their predecessors. They experienced Post Traumatic Stress Disorder and trauma on a grand scale. The third wave came through the "Orderly Departure Program", structured by the United Nations High Commissioner for Refugees, or UNHCR. The Program was created to help provide a safe and structured method of getting refugees to resettlement. These waves of newcomers make up vastly different demographics in terms of experiences, levels of trauma, connections and financial resources. Refugees sometimes face resistance by their new neighbors and are often seen as a drain on resources. These neighbors in the host country may want to remember that those who have fled and survived also bring resilience, strength and the hope for a better future for their children, just as scores of immigrants who preceded them.

Not all of the stories of recent immigrants are dismal, some are inspiring, and others have traces of humor. Shoua relates the story of an older Hmong gentleman new to America who spoke no English. One day he was in town shopping and became very thirsty. He looked around until he observed a younger man leaning over a rectangular silver-metal box and water arced out. When the young man stepped aside, the older gentleman approached, happy to have found water. He leaned over the box as he'd seen the other man do – nothing happened. He stepped back, confused (and still thirsty) to observe again. A second young man stepped forth, his hands clasped behind his back, leaned over and drank from the arc of water. The older man thought, "ah-hah!" When it was his turn, he too clasped his hands behind his back and leaned forward. No water. "Perhaps this only works for white people," he thought, frustrated, wondering how the box knew he was Asian. He was about ready to kick the metal box as he stood aside and watched a third man approach. This time he noticed the foot petal the man stepped on to activate the water and the older gentleman was finally able to quench his thirst.

Another story involved an elderly lady from Laos who immigrated to the United States and surprised her son and daughter when they came home from work by having rice already made for dinner. The aged woman had previously struggled to learn how to use light switches, water taps and other seemingly basic American contraptions, so her ability to cook rice surprised them greatly. "Mom!" they cried. "How did you get the rice cooked? Where did you find water?"

"Over there," the old woman stated, and led them to a bowl full of water…. The toilet.

Shoua would face his own challenges and opportunities in his new country.

Chapter 10
Arrival in the United States and College Years

After the long flight on Continental Airlines, Shoua arrived in San Francisco, the port of entry for so many Asian born immigrants and refugees. As he looked around at the rows of plastic seats and jumped at the sound of the overhead paging system, he felt his senses over stimulated and a deep exhaustion from the long journey. Just then, a young man who was a refugee navigator offered to help carry Shoua's bags through the airport. Thinking he was trustworthy; Shoua gratefully accepted his help. He was, after all, very tired and overwhelmed after his long flights. Moments later, walking through the busy terminal, Shoua lost sight of his alleged benefactor. Shoua broke into a jog, straining to see where the man had gone. There was no sign of him or the white bag that all refugees were given, the bag with a drawing of a man and woman on it. The man had taken what few possessions Shoua owned, including his identification and travel documents. Shoua was a crime victim within minutes of his arrival in America. Ironically, Shoua had recently sworn an oath to not commit any crimes upon entering the United States and had solemnly promised to be an upstanding citizen. This same adolescent boy had been robbed upon entry into the country. He now had no transfer ticket to get to Denver where his brother lived and in the days of paperless e-tickets it meant he was - once again- left waiting. He found himself in limbo for almost a week as he waited for another transfer ticket to be issued.

During the wait Shoua stayed in a hotel room near the airbase. He stared out of the window at the four-lane highway and marveled at the number of cars–they were going *so* fast! He looked around his room, soaking it all in. The room contained many wonders. Carpeting, not brushed dirt floors. A bed, not a bamboo mat. Light with just the flick of a switch. Indoor plumbing and flush toilets. Running water- no digging deep holes and having to wait for the debris to settle before drinking. Television! Shoua ate the rice and boiled meat supplied by the refugee coordinators and shrugged into the jacket they'd supplied him to ward off the chilly San Francisco night air. He pushed the curtain aside and gazed once again out of the window. It was so clean here! He recalled the paper littering the refugee camps and the human waste everywhere, the stench and the overcrowded feeling. As he observed his new surroundings, he took in the vast amount of concrete. Where were all the trees in America? He was used to farmlands and forests. This cement jungle may take some getting used to.

Shoua felt a tremendous sense of relief to no longer be in the camps. He felt clean and free. "I don't know what my future will hold," he thought. "But I'm in America!" His next sentiment was, "I don't have my parents". He lay on the big bed in his hotel room and fought back the tears of his conflicted emotions. Fear and hope, loneliness and excitement all tumbled together in his mind. He was homesick for his village and at the same time so immensely relieved to no longer be trapped in the camp, anxious to be reunited with his brother but nervous about his new life in Denver. The mental exhaustion eventually took its toll and Shoua rolled into a ball for a nap.

When he awoke he sat on the edge of his bed, his arms wrapped around his bony knees. "When you're free you do a lot of think-ing", Shoua explained years later. He thought about his parents, and the sister and niece he had left behind, the armed guards and barbed wire fences and the family that had taken him in at the camp. He watched the headlamps from the highway- the long stream of bright lights heading in one direction and a long stream of red in the other. He wondered where all of these people of America were heading and what was their rush? He marveled at so much of humanity trapped in their expensive metal boxes. Shoua's thoughts were interrupted by a knock on the door. He unfolded his small frame and opened the door, too small to check the peek hole. There stood the official in charge of his relocation proceedings. She smiled with the good news that the replacement transfer ticket had finally been issued. Shoua would soon be on the last leg of the journey to his new home in Denver, Colorado.

Since his transfer ticket had been stolen, no one was sure which flight Shoua would be on or when he would arrive in Denver. As a result, Shoua's brother-and sister-in-law were at work when his flight touched down and there was no family member to greet him at the airport. Instead, he was received by a refugee services worker. Since the worker knew Shoua's brother Vang, he took Shoua to his own home for a few hours until Vang got off work and could pick Shoua up and take him to his new home in America, a small, converted garage in north Denver. When Shoua and his brother were reunited, the tears fell unabashedly as the brothers, long separated, embraced.

Shoua recalls his first trip to an American grocery store. He had never shopped for food indoors before, as markets are open air where he comes from. He looked with wonder at the aisle full of frozen foods–how amazing! He found the prices staggering and the entire experience to be completely different from anything he was used to. Years later, Shoua observed how quickly the grocery stores ran out of food after a severe storm in Denver. It occurred to him that if war ever broke out in America there would not be a lot of options for obtaining food. When he lived in the village in the mountains of Laos, he and his family ate the food they harvested, picked fresh fruit from the trees and butchered the animals they raised. In the US, aside from a small plot in the back garden, people were not so self-reliant.

One of the things Shoua missed the most was the feel of standing next to a hot fire in the morning. While he could put on a jacket or raise the heat in their small home when he felt the early morning chill, that couldn't replace the sense of comfort and community he experienced when everyone started their day drawn to a central location and experience. It was a naked feeling. The closest comparison to western culture may be not starting the day with a hot cup of tea or coffee with a loved one. The fire was a central component of the family, and he missed the experience deeply.

Vang and his wife Va lived in a predominantly white area in Denver. Vang was concerned about Shoua developing identity issues, as he would have been one of the only Asian students in the neighborhood school. As a result, Vang sent Shoua to live with a cousin in a more diverse part of town. Federal Boulevard, directly west of Denver, is home to a large number of Latino and Asian families. The street is lined with Vietnamese grocery stores and Mexican restaurants. Shoua lived with his cousin in the housing projects and attended Kepner Middle School (coincidentally, the author worked at Kepner as a substance abuse counselor fifteen years later. It was not until one of our interviews that this connection was made). Shoua struggled to learn the language of his new country. English is his third language after Hmong and Lao. He attended English as a Second Language (ESL) classes and math, taught in English.

The housing unit in which Shoua lived with his cousins was surrounded by large, old oak trees. Shoua was amazed as he watched the leaves change colors and fall off in autumn, leaving the tree bare, only to re-bloom in the spring. He had never experienced a change of seasons, and the newness interested him. He found that the effect of the bare trees in winter created the illusion of a lonely place where all of the trees were dead. Used to the jungle, which was perpetually green, lush, and flowering, he found the effect depressing. To this day, late fall and winter are Shoua's least favorite seasons. The trees by the housing projects were home to many grey squirrels scampering up and down the bumpy bark. Shoua reminisced about the time he and a cousin were startled by a squirrel in the jungle and were desperate to shoot it, they were so ravenous. The boys had been unable to fire their weapon due to the loud report it would have made, so they could only watch the creature jump to the next branch. Now here he was, gazing up into trees, the home to so many squirrels and birds. If Americans had any idea how he used to delight in catching them, how pleased he was to get some degree of nourishment into his belly, they would be amazed, he thought.

Shoua bolted up in bed, suppressing a scream and struggling with his blankets. Shoua had had the nightmare... again. In it, he traveled to Laos to visit relatives and was unable to find his way home. He was stuck in the country of his birth, not able to escape to the country he now calls home. Any path he tried would lead him in circles, seemingly farther and farther from home. When he awakened, confusion wore on him like his heavy blanket. *Was* he in Laos? He took account of his surroundings; he had a pillow under his head and he was in a warm, comfortable bed. He was in America! Shoua had this recurring nightmare for the first three or four years of his life in the United States. One night he dreamt he had been visiting family back in Laos and was ready to return home. In the dream, he crossed here, made a turn there, made his way to Thailand and then to the US- it seemed so easy! Interestingly, after the dream in which he figured out his way back to the US, he never again had the nightmare about getting stuck and lost in Laos.

When Shoua completed middle school (then "junior high"), Shoua moved back in with his brother and sister-in-law and attended Highland High School in north Denver. There, as one of the only Asian students in the entire school, he was called "Bruce Lee" by his white peers.

Refugees have remarked on the overwhelming changes they encounter so abruptly. *Everything* is different- the food, language, housing, values, technology, plants, currency, and climate. Many refugees who have been relocated to another part of the globe struggle with the extreme changes in temperatures they face. People who have relocated from such countries as the Congo, Sudan, and Iraq share their experiences as they find themselves living in Minnesota or Colorado, sometimes moving there in the dead of winter. Not only do they lack the appropriate gear for wintertime (coats, boots, gloves, etc.), but their arrival marks the first time many of them have ever seen snow. One refugee from a hot climate joked that she would have loved to have been relocated to Florida, but she wasn't given the choice. Another man shared that his daughter contracted pneumonia when the family was settled in Colorado in the middle of winter and they had none of the appropriate cold weather gear. Fortunately for Shoua, Colorado wasn't as severe a change as one might expect. The mountains of northern Laos get very cold, especially at night, so his transition to the climate wasn't as drastic as it could have been.

Shoua's sister Sue was chatting and catching up with the white woman who was helping her transition to life in America. Sue complained about the toilets in the US, explaining that she had to wash her feet every time before using them. Confused, the woman followed Sue into the restroom and had her demonstrate (clothed) how she used the toilet. Sue stood on the porcelain seat and squatted, Thai and Lao style. The woman chuckled and showed Sue how to sit on a western style toilet. In Southeast Asia people squat on a porcelain structure, feet straddling the hole. It is easy to see how a person could be confused with a similar, yet very different, technology. Americans who visit Southeast Asia often leave those toilets with a confused expression. "What do I do with that bucket of water and the ladle? Where is the toilet paper?" Cultural context takes on an interesting twist.

Figure 1, Toilets in Southeast Asia are used by standing on the white, flat ceramic and straddling the small bowl. It is easy to see how people relocated to the US thought they should stand on the toilet seat. Photo taken by author

Shoua was exposed to a multitude of different experiences, cultural practices, and people (he recalls seeing a black person for the first time), during his first years in America. He was enchanted with the new foods he encountered in the west. Used to a diet consisting mostly of rice or noodles and vegetables, he now was exposed to hamburgers, pizza, and fried chicken. Even the housing was foreign to him. Having the stove and cooking area, running water and bathroom all inside the house were new experiences. One interesting observation made by a Hmong refugee is the need for money in the United States. If you need food, medicine, or shelter in the jungle, you simply grow it, pick it or make it. You don't need money for much. That is about the only thing that's easier there (Laos) than here (the US).

Shoua was surprised to learn that many students in the US are allowed to dress however they'd like- most don't have to wear uniforms as he was used to. Nor do students demonstrate the type of respect for teachers as they do in his homeland. Students in Laos rise when their teacher enters a room, much like attendees do in court when the judge arrives. Teachers in the US aren't allowed to hit students as they did at home, where the teacher was expected to take over for the parents once children entered the school building. In the Hmong culture, direct eye contact is considered rude and inappropriate and is therefore avoided. This is obviously problematic when an American teacher, school administrator or other person of authority misinterprets the downcast eyes of the student as being evasive, painfully shy, or deceitful.

People in the United States come from a low context model, meaning they say what they mean and are typically very direct. Shoua was shocked to discover that people will tell you to your face if they don't like you. In Hmong culture, people will often say "maybe" or "I will try" rather than the direct and seemingly rude "no" response that is accepted in the west. (One therapist in Denver learned this lesson the hard way. When she set up appointments with her clients from Africa, they failed to show up. She then learned that they were culturally bound to answer "yes" to any offer or be considered rude. As a result, she changed her strategy from asking, "Would you like to come in for another appointment?" to, "Would you like to have your appointment in a week, two weeks or would you like to call me when you are ready?")

Asian culture tends to be indirect, using a high context model. For example, in some traditional Korean exchanges, a guest is offered a cup of tea. The guest knows to refuse the cup, not wanting to be a nuisance. The host offers a second time, and again the guest politely turns it down. When the host offers tea for the third time, the guest happily accepts, having established that they are not inconveniencing the host. It is a cultural dance, the asking three times before the eventual acceptance. The west operates using low context; if you want a cup of tea, you say yes. If you don't, you say no. It doesn't take much imagination to appreciate the offense that might be taken when the two traditions collide. Many Hmong beliefs are similar to those of other Asian cultures, including, according to a 2001 study, "collectivism, conformity to norms, deference to authority figures, emotional restraint, filial piety (respect and care for one's parents and elders), hierarchical family structure, and humility... recently immigrated first generation Asian-Americans will adhere to these values more strongly than will Asian-Americans who are many generations removed from immigration." While the Hmong are a unique cultural identity unto themselves, they fit into many of the overarching themes found in other Asian societies.

In high school, Shoua worked hard to catch up with the academic level of his peers, as Hmong who live in the high mountains of Laos typically don't receive rigorous education. Shoua had been fending off starvation for years, not hitting the books. He actually asked his school academic counselor to be held back a year so he would have more time to learn the language and catch up with the other students. The counselor denied his request, explaining that he had passed all of his courses, received excellent feedback from teachers in regards to his work ethic and academic effort, and in fact qualified to graduate a semester *early*.

The school brought in a Hmong counselor to come to the high school to talk with Shoua about his academic future and help him prepare his application for college. The counselor recommended Shoua attend a community college. Shoua decided, to the disappointment of the counselor, to take a year off. When he did apply to attend higher education, it was to a four-year state college.

Shoua entered Metropolitan State College of Denver (now a University) and did well his freshman year. "Metro" is an urban commuter campus, unusual in that it is not a traditional dormitory style college. Shoua, like most students attending Metro, lived at home with family and scheduled work around classes and studying. He lived with his brother, Vang and sister-in-law, Va and drove a red Buick they gave him to help with transportation to his work and classes. They all worked. Shoua spent his after-school hours at Church's Chicken where he was a cashier and fry cook and eventually a team leader, responsible for inventory and deposits. Vang labored at a factory job making rebar and Va worked at a factory sewing uniforms for cheerleaders. Despite this effort, the family still relied on food stamps to survive and found themselves having to reapply every six months to qualify. Vang and his wife could speak English but could not read or write in that language, so it became Shoua's job to understand the confusing bureaucracy required to renew their application. Interestingly, this skill came in handy when Shoua would one day help his future clients apply for welfare, food stamps and negotiate the social services system in his work as a victim's advocate.

At the beginning of Shoua's second year in college, Vang was diagnosed with neck cancer and spent the better part of that year in and out of the hospital for evaluations and treatment. Shoua adjusted his school and work schedule to accommodate his family. Shoua would take his sister-in-law to work, head to class, then pick her up and take her to the hospital for visitation. Shoua then went to work before picking her up again and taking her home. He would arrive to class early, trying to use any spare precious moments he could capture to study. Shoua tried to read his textbooks and review notes before his colleagues arrived to fill up the classroom and classes started. Because of the disruption to his studies caused by ferrying Va, Shoua failed his second year of college and dropped out when his brother died. Perhaps as a distraction from his loss, Shoua took on an extra job at a warehouse, unloading boxed shipments and taking inventory. Shoua was private and stoic about the loss of his brother as he had been when his father and mother starved to death in the jungles of Laos.

For many years, one of Shoua's biggest regrets was not being with Vang when he passed away. Shoua had spent time visiting him at the hospital, but was also very busy with work, attending classes, catching up on reading, homework and assignments as well as driving Va around. When Vang took his last breath on earth, Shoua was not able to be there and had no opportunity to say his final goodbye. The regret burned into him as real as any cinder on his flesh. One night, Shoua had a dream. Vang was sick in the hospital, wearing a thin gown and sporting medical tubes from his arms. In the dream, Shoua held his big brother and patted his head. He told Vang he loved him and was there with him, holding him in Vang's final moments. The dream was very healing for Shoua; when he awoke, he felt lighter. He no longer carries the burden of regret. (In another of his fascinating dreams, Shoua saw the winning numbers to a state lottery contest. He awoke, remembering all five of the numbers he had seen in his vision [there are six in the lottery]. He padded to the kitchen for a drink of water determined to write the numbers down in the morning, as he certainly had a clear memory of the digits. He went back to bed and fell asleep. When he awakened at dawn, the numbers, so firmly ensconced in his brain during the wee hours of the night had disappeared! He cursed himself for not having written them down. That night, as he watched the evening news anchor announce the five out of six numbers, *his dreamt numbers*, he shook his head in disbelief.)

It is customary in Hmong culture (and some Middle Eastern cultures) for a man to marry the wife of his deceased brother to help take care of her and any children she may have. This practice, called levirate, would only occur in Hmong culture between the widow and a younger brother of her deceased husband, never an older brother. Thus it was expected of remaining aunts and uncles (who were living in California but still very much a part of the decision making in the family) that Shoua marry Vang's wife to help protect and support her. Shoua was nineteen years old and the baby of the family, and his sister-in-law was significantly older. She looked and acted more like a mother to Shoua than a wife, and he couldn't imagine being wed to a woman with whom he felt more maternal love than romantic. When Shoua explained to Va that he couldn't marry her, she felt he had dishonored her by breaking with tradition and kicked him out of the house.

Shoua, nineteen years old, now had to find a place to live, make major decisions about his future, education & career, and discover how to make a place for himself in the world. On his own. While grieving. As he had done with other challenges in his life, Shoua simply got it done. He found a one-bedroom apartment for the 1980s rate of $315 a month and found a higher paying job at an electronics firm soldering parts and packaging large floppy disks. He met with an admissions counselor at Metropolitan State College of Denver and together they explained to the office of financial aid the circumstances behind Shoua's failed sophomore year. He was granted a second chance. Shoua once again applied himself to his studies, excelling in math and social work courses. While attending classes, he landed a job at the college in Accounts Payable as a work study in order to make more money. One of his responsibilities was to ferry checks from one building to the next for processing. Shoua recalls one day he was carrying over two million dollars' worth of checks in a manila envelope. His boss instructed him not to talk to anyone and then called the receptionist in the building where Shoua was headed, so they knew to expect him. Shoua nervously carried over the deposit, fighting the paranoia a person naturally feels in such a situation. When he arrived, the receptionist called the boss to confirm his safe arrival; the manila envelope and its valuable contents had made it. This made for an interesting twist. Shoua came from a culture where money was not required for survival, to one that bases all worth around it, and found himself employed in the very department that accepts and transfers money. He eventually left that job for the higher paying role of a health care financial administrator with US Health and Human Services where he was responsible for quality control of Medicaid. He especially liked the convenience of his new job, as it was within walking distance of classes. He later landed an internship at the Asian Pacific Development Center (APDC), an agency that specialized in assisting Asian immigrants and refugees who have experienced violence or trauma.

Against all odds, Shoua graduated in 1993 with a bachelor's degree in social work. He was hired by APDC as a part time mental health clinician, where he worked for many years. Shoua then rose to the position of Victims Assistance Services Project Director. APDC provides a number of services for the refugee and immigrant community. They offer English as a Second Language (ESL) classes, computer/technical support, and legal support including victim assistance, a youth program, translation and interpretation services, babysitting, a medical clinic, psychiatric care and even a community garden. Classes are offered to help with job readiness and becoming a citizen. Programs assist clients with everything from copyrights and patents to college admission forms, from depositions and polygraph screenings to tourism events. Amongst its varying staff members, the agency can communicate in 32 languages, including Akhan, Urdu, Farsi and Amharic. All staff members speak English and at least one Asian language; Shoua speaks Hmong, Lao and English.

Outside of each office is a small machine making "white noise" so the conversations of the crime victims and survivors of domestic violence and assault cannot be overheard and will remain confidential. A significant part of Shoua's job at APDC was to provide support for victims of crime and domestic violence. This involved educating his clients about crimes covered by the Victim Rights Act, accompanying them to court, helping them with access to Victim Compensation Assistance and providing the link to any mental health and legal services they may need. If anyone has an understanding of trauma and victimization, it would be Shoua.

Shoua found his work at APDC in parts challenging, frustrating and fulfilling. While he enjoyed providing assistance to those in need, his life as a man married to his work would soon change in ways Shoua did not expect.

Chapter 11
Building a life,
Finding a Wife.

The short version of Shoua's marriage is summed up when he explains, "I met my wife in the morning, and I married her in the afternoon." The full version is even more interesting. When Shoua was in his early thirties, his family decided it was time for him to marry. Traditionally in Hmong culture the father makes the decision of when a young man should enter into matrimony, but because his father was deceased, Shoua's cousin stepped in and fulfilled that role. It was arranged for Shoua to marry his uncle's third wife's daughter. The uncle had brought his three wives to the US with him. He claimed one as his wife, another as a sister and the third as a cousin (the uncle must have had the means to be able to pay the bride price for three different wives). The uncle told the young woman about Shoua, her new husband-to-be. "He goes to school and studies very hard. He has a clean apartment and is a good kid." The young woman had a boyfriend and was not interested in marriage to a man she had never met, but she followed Hmong tradition which demands obedience from daughters. Shoua flew to Fresno, California to fetch her and bring her back to Denver where they found they didn't care for each other at all. Her heart belonged to another, and Shoua found he was not attracted to her, either. Their relationship felt decidedly more like a brother-sister arrangement than that of husband and wife. After a month of living like siblings, one sleeping on the bed the other the couch, he returned her to his uncle in California. The two-hour flight felt significantly longer due to the awkward silence between them. Shoua and his non-bride felt badly that the arranged union didn't work out and fervently hoped they hadn't disappointed their family. They both felt, however, there was simply nothing between them that would keep them happily bound together. The uncle was disappointed and angry at the young woman, which allowed Shoua to save face, an important construct in many Asian cultures. If Shoua had been to blame, he would have dishonored his family. If the fault did not lie with him, however, he could retain his integrity with the family. Additionally, as there had never been a legally recognized US marriage ceremony or documents filed, no official annulment or divorce was necessary. Shoua remained single for years after that, focusing on his work with refugees and victims of violence. Eventually the topic of marriage resurfaced.

It was not important to Shoua what race his future wife might be. He was not particularly concerned with finding someone who was from Laos or who, more specifically, was Hmong. This was a very important trait to his uncle and brother, however, who convinced 38-year-old Shoua that because he was the last living male relative with the 'Her' last name, he should keep up the family line with a wife from his cultural background. The uncle explained to Shoua, simply, "You're getting old. It's time for you to find a wife and start a family." The unspoken message was that Shoua should have a son, as male heirs not only carry on the family name but are the ones who take care of their aging parents and guide the parents' spirits to rest after they die.

Shoua conceded to be married. His cousin showed Shoua a recently made video called, "Pretty Hmong Girls in the New Year", which displayed girls from various villages enjoying local festivals. Shoua saw a girl he liked on the video and learned her name. Armed solely with that information, he traveled to Laos to find her. He didn't know the name of her village or even in what part of the country she lived- he had only the memory of her face and her name! Luckily, her last name was not Her, but Thao. In the Hmong tradition, strangers cannot marry if they hold the same family name as it is considered taboo to marry within a clan. Ironically, this means that first cousins can marry if they have different last names, as they are from differing clans. Shoua knew that the most opportune time to meet this woman, if he were able to find her at all, would be during the New Year's Celebration. Interestingly, Shoua had a strong gut feeling that he would meet his wife at the last minute.

The celebration of New Years is a major holiday for the Hmong community. It is the time to acknowledge that the old year has passed and welcome in the new. The festivities are much more elaborate than the west's version of listening to Auld Lang Syne and popping open a bottle of champagne. Rather, entire communities come together to eat, play games, and meet their future life partners. Some Hmong communities in major US cities are beginning to adopt a Westernized version of their holiday including carnival rides, food vendors and beauty pageants but in the old country traditions remain strong. During this enormous social event, it is thought that having good food will help ensure having good fortune in the New Year, so chickens and pig are butchered for the feast. Revelers eat sticky rice patties which are first offered to ancestral spirits. It is a joyous time, and a time to, according to Cha Po's An Introduction to Hmong Culture, "avoid all conflicts, ill behaviors and bad deeds". It is also the time for young people to put down the hoe and other farming implements and socialize, flirt, court and find a husband or wife. They participate in a ball toss, standing in a line with girls on one side and boys on the other, throwing a ball made of cotton or silk or even of clothes that have been wrapped tightly together to form a ball. The ball is tossed to the opposing person, some-one of the opposite gender. If someone drops the ball, he or she has to sing a song chosen by the other person or hand over an ornament from his or her costume. This playful courting ritual is also accompanied by reciting poetry. These activities give the young people an opportunity to see each other, chat and flirt and decide if the person near them might be a suitable mate.

The revelers wear festive garb, special outfits the women spend months embroidering (delete for months), specifically for the New Year's Celebrations. Girls wear heavy, intricate silver necklaces. They would have received their first one as a baby during the ceremony celebrating the survival of the first thirty days of life (due to the high mortality rate, the thirty-day period marked an important milestone). More silver is added to the necklace each year until it hangs almost to the waist and weighs around five pounds. The jewelry is sometimes one of the few valued possessions the family owns as traditionally the family would have accumulated their wealth in silver bars and/or these necklaces. The girls and women would wear the basic silver necklaces at all times, even when working in the fields, but would only add the fancy ornaments during special occasions such as New Years. Some households sell opium poppies as a cash crop to buy the silver used to make the jewelry. The necklaces represent wealth and beauty, and if a family is so poor they can't afford one, they borrow one for their daughter to wear during the festivities. "Historically, Hmong families had few material possessions due to their semi-nomadic lifestyle. Her clothing was the only thing a woman would have taken when she married and moved away from her home village. It was, therefore, her identity, indicating ethnicity, displaying wealth, and advertising the wifely credentials of creativity, patience and diligence. The necklace has three sao or 'locks', symbolizing locking the soul in the body. Traditionally made of silver, nowadays, few families can afford them and it's more common to see aluminum."

Figure 1, Hmong women wear heavy, elaborate silver necklaces for the New Year and during wedding celebrations.
Photo taken by author with permission from the Hmong Cultural Center, St. Paul, Minnesota

Figure 2, Due to the cost of silver, many Hmong necklaces are now made from aluminum such as the one above.
Photo taken by author with permission at The Traditional Arts and Ethnology Centre (TAEC) in Luang Prabang, Laos

There were two major cities in Laos celebrating New Years. Shoua went to one city to meet girls, and his cousin, energetic in his attempts to find Shoua a mate, visited the other city. There he filmed the girls lined up for the traditional Hmong courting ritual of the ball toss and showed the footage to Shoua when they met up later that evening. The cousin asked, "Which one do you like?" "Nobody" was Shoua's stubborn reply. He was still hopeful he would see "Ge", the girl from the original video footage.

Over the next few days, many girls were interested in Shoua, but he did not fancy them. He also courted and proposed to several young women, only to be rejected. He felt pressured to meet someone and rushed in his search. The intuitive feeling that he would meet his future wife at the last moment persisted as he searched for a mate. It may surprise readers to learn that

Shoua (and other Hmong men) propose to the women they just met. Shoua explains that in the United States people date for a long time before getting married, "And then you already know everything about the person!" He prefers the Hmong tradition of marrying someone you like and then spending the rest of your life getting to know them. He gently explains that the relationship lasts longer because you have so much to learn and experience with this new person. After a month of attending New Year's celebrations and looking for the girl from the video, Shoua had run out of time. The moment of his return flight to the United States was quickly approaching. Shoua prepared to spend his last day doing laundry, packing, and resting. He was very tired from (please remove 'spent') commuting between the two cities, participating in the festivities and from the emotional turbulence of his trip. On his last night, his cousin was adamant that he drive to Kilometer 52, one of the main cities in which the festivities were being held. Shoua declined, explaining his exhaustion. "Come on, Uncle-Come with me!" his cousin begged, invoking the deferential term "Uncle" out of respect for his older cousin. Through his cousin's sheer persistence, Shoua made the two-hour drive back out to Kilometer 52 to participate in the end of the New Year's activities. The two men, enjoying the festivities, walked around and looked at the vendors' tables displaying handicrafts for sale. They smelled thin slices of beef drying in the sun and heard cracklings popping in hot oil. At the food stalls, Shoua looked for a stall selling bee larvae. He preferred the big ones, the larvae that were almost the size of a full grown bee, not the tiny ones. He bought some fried fish and a Pepsi, and his cousin had boiled chicken, sticky rice and cold water. They dug in their pockets for 1,000 kip (Lao currency, pronounced "keep") needed to use the restroom facilities. Then, as he was about to leave the green space of the park, Shoua saw her out of the corner of his eye- the girl from the video. This young woman, whom he had never met but had been searching for, had also nearly missed the last night of ceremonies because she was tired but *her* cousin had pushed and cajoled her into attending. Had either Shoua or this girl succumbed to feeling tired, or if either of the cousins been less relentless, Shoua may have never met the woman who was to become his wife.

Figure 3, Shoua and Ge when they first met during the New Years Celebrations in Laos
Photo courtesy of Shoua Her

"Ge?" he asked as he approached the girl he had been seeking.

"How do you know my name?" she asked shyly. Shoua explained the video and his search for her. It turns out she had been at the festivities every day and he had somehow missed her until his last afternoon in Laos. Shoua and Ge (pronounced "G") participated in the traditional ball toss with a decidedly untraditional tennis ball in place of a cotton one. They shared a Pepsi before Shoua worked up the nerve to ask Ge if they could go to her house. It is traditional for the families to meet and gather when the male proposes to a female. Females do not propose marriage. The new couple would not have held hands, as girlfriends and boyfriends do not display affection publicly. Once in the home, with family members present and chickens running about, Shoua asked tentatively, "I want to marry you. Are you ok?" "I am ok." With that, they were engaged. Immediately after she said yes to Shoua's proposal, the rooster in the house crowed twice, a very auspicious sign for the new couple. Ge's cousin later said he had never heard the rooster do that before at that time of day and he took it as a very positive message. Shoua discretely asked the neighbors about Ge. Was she a good Hmong girl or did she run around? Did she care for her parents? Was she respectful of her elders? The neighbors vetted Ge. While she wasn't home much, traveling for singing performances, she was good to her parents. Shoua was satisfied. He then offered Ge's parents money for a dowry, or "bride price". In the old country, Shoua and his family would have offered silver bars to the bride's family. Many cultures pay a dowry to the groom's family when a wedding takes place, but Hmong culture offers money to the bride's family instead, to help compensate the family for raising a daughter worthy of marriage. This can be problematic when a man feels as if he has "bought" his wife, but Shoua accepted the tradition and paid the bride price. He offered $4,500, higher than the more traditional $2,000 that was often paid at the time. $500 was to be used for the wedding and the extra was intended for the family, as they would be helping to care for her while he arranged for her entry to the United States.

Shoua is a "Blue" Hmong, Ge a "White" Hmong. While there are other variations, including Green, Striped and Flowery, Blue and White are the major types. One of the biggest differences between a "Blue" and "White" Hmong is the language dialect. The differences in dialect have been compared to speaking a British version of English vs. a New York version of the same language. Another major difference between the two groups is the traditional dress. Women who are Blue Hmong tend to wear more colorful dresses made of hemp (the leaves of the marijuana plant are thrown away; only the hemp material is used) and decorated with embroidery. Batik is applied after beeswax, collected by the village men, delineates the pattern and the material is dyed in indigo. After the skirt is boiled, the color and designs stay and the wax melts away. Some clothing is decorated with coins left over from the French occupation era (landowners find it easier to hire some hill tribe laborers if they pay in Indochinese coins rather than cash, for this reason). Traditionally, the women used natural elements to create the colors in cloth. Green hues were created using the bark from mango and Indian almond trees, neem and cassia leaves. Malayana olive trees were used for greys and jackfruit wood, mango leaves, turmeric and Indian trumpet flowers for yellows.

Blue Hmong men wear very long pants and a white shirt that ends midriff. Shoua shares the story that many years ago the Chinese would grab the men's shirts while the Hmong were trying to escape capture. The men began shortening their shirts to give the enemy less material to grab onto. They have maintained the style ever since. The difference in the subgroups (Blue Hmong vs. White) did not prove to be a problem for the new couple.

Figure 4, Shoua explains that many years ago the Chinese would grab the men's shirts while the Hmong were trying to escape capture. The men began shortening their shirts to give the enemy less material to grab onto. They have maintained the style ever since.
Photo taken by author with permission from the Hmong Cultural Center, St. Paul, Minnesota

Figure 5, Traditional White Hmong women
Photo from the Laos National Museum, Vientiane, Laos, used with
permission.

Figure 6, Ge "Mai" Her in Blue Hmong skirt (this would be worn at
New Year's celebrations)
Photo courtesy of Shoua Her

Figure 7, Ge "Mai" posing in a White Hmong traditional skirt
Photo courtesy of Shoua Her

When it is decided that a couple is to be married, it is the job of negotiators to make the arrangements for the bride price, to be paid on the day of the wedding. Families do not discuss the issue with each other in order to save face if the arrangements do not come together. Because Shoua's parents were deceased, he needed to find a surrogate family to step in for him and arrange a negotiator. It is the negotiator's role to come up with a bride price that is affordable (but still substantial) from the groom's family. The groom then brings a gift of dried tobacco, now offered in the form of cigarettes, to the bride's family as a token of appreciation and to start the discussion and negotiations that accompany the union. Shoua offered Ge's family two cigarettes, which are accepted whether or not the family smokes. The offer must be of two cigarettes, not one, or superstition dictates that a death will soon follow. Shoua also offered two little cups of drink -soda or alcohol are the modern acceptable beverages- on the living room table.

Figure 8, The negotiators for the engagement included a shaman, two men to represent Ge (on the left) and two men to represent Shoua (on the right).
Photo courtesy of Shoua Her

Under Shaman tradition, when a girl comes into a boy's house to live, the spirit must accept her. The boy's family uses a live chicken to tell the spirit, "These are my people, not strangers. Don't make this girl sick – she's part of our family now". A rooster may be swung around the new wife's head three times to keep her ancestors from making trouble, before being sacrificed for the spirit. Shoua didn't follow this practice, as he is a Christian Hmong. He did participate in a traditional Hmong wedding, however, which is a celebration of joining two families and clans together and an acknowledgement that the wife goes from being directed and disciplined by her family to that of her husband.

Traditional Hmong wedding ceremonies usually last for two days. Family representatives negotiate gifts, prepare mounds of food and lecture the new couple on the principles of matrimony. Chickens and pigs are slaughtered for the feast and tables are laden with steaming bowls of rice, bamboo shoots and vegetables. The bride and groom-to-be visit each family's house and the traditional wedding song is performed. After the blessings and songs are completed, the couple is considered married and the groom is given a ceremonial wedding umbrella and the bride a *siv cib*, or a black and white striped cloth. In Hmong legend, these items came from *Zaj Laug*, The Old Dragon, and represent protection and blessings. They are thought to shield the couple from harm. Finally, the couple kowtows to the various parents, aunts, uncles and cousins in attendance and the ceremony is considered complete. Because Shoua and Ge's wedding took place with so little notice and because he had a flight to catch, however, their ceremony was abbreviated.

According to a description in the book *Hmong and American; From Refugees to Citizens*, the following scene is likely to have taken place before the wedding of Shoua and Ge. One of the women would have grabbed a knife and a bowl and disappeared into the backyard where she would have spotted one of the plump chickens scratching in the dirt. She would have grabbed the bird and pulled both wings behind its back, tying them in a knot with one hand and grabbing the claws together with the other. She would have tucked the claws behind the knotted wings and plucked the feathers from the bird before quickly slicing open the chicken's throat, catching the blood in a bowl to make blood chicken salad. The women in the family would have prepared the wedding feast, and when the meal was ready, they would have stood behind the men as they ate, waiting to refill glasses of rice whiskey and plates of food. It was only when the men finished eating that the women would sit down to eat the remaining food before they began to clean the mess made by the wedding revelers.

Shoua met Ge at 10 in the morning. By noon he was at the house, meeting the family and by 5:00 that evening he and Ge were married. He left the village at midnight for the two-hour drive back to the capital in order to catch his noon flight back to the United States. Traditionally, Shoua and his bride would have moved in with his parents where the couple would live for several years before beginning a life of their own. The cultural landscape had shifted considerably, however, since Shoua's parents started their lives as a young married couple. Since then, a war had ravaged their homeland, they both had perished due to starvation and Shoua had begun a new life in America. He met his bride at a much later age than Hmong custom dictated. While all of these elements did not deter the newlyweds from their efforts at a happy reunion, there would be a delay in the beginning of their life together. Shoua had to leave his new bride in Laos where she would stay with his cousin while he returned alone to the United States. Shoua spent the next several months filling out forms for a fiancée visa, as his Hmong marriage was not a recognized legal US ceremony. Only then could be bring Ge to the US to live with him in Denver. Shoua takes great pride in the fact that he completed these documents without an attorney's help. The name Ge did not appear in the family registry; perhaps because of the turmoil of war, that detail was overlooked. It would be very difficult to apply for documentation to the US without that registration, so Ge took on the name of her sister who had died. Ge became "Mai" (pronounced "My"), and suddenly found herself officially two years older. By taking on the identity of her sister who was registered, it was much easier to process her paperwork. Ge was granted a temporary, two-year green card which would be modified as her marital status changed.

Figure 9, Shoua and Ge ("Mai") at their US ceremony in a Hmong Church in Westminster, Colorado.
Photo courtesy of Shoua Her

In Hmong tradition, the parents of the bride bestow upon their son-in-law his new "adult name", the name by which he would be known henceforth, after the birth of the couple's first child. (Green Hmong's tradition dictates that the husband's parents decide his new adult name). Thus, Shoua's cousin, Doua Her, became Cher Doua Her (and if he still lived in the highlands of Laos, he would be known by his clan name first). Mai's parents gave Shoua the name Cha, so he would have been known as Cha Shoua Her. Shoua respectfully declined going by his new name, however, gently explaining to his in-laws that his mother had given him that name after her own brother (culturally, it was accepted for Hmong to change either their given name or their new adult name to overcome misfortune so it would not have been unheard of for Shoua to keep his given name). The uncle for whom Shoua had been named was very patient and generous, and it was special to have been named after him. What Shoua didn't mention was that the name he was given at birth helped him to feel connected to his mother, now deceased. He also reasoned to himself that his in-laws lived far away and wouldn't know what name he used in America.

If Shoua and Ge (now Mai) practiced Shamanism, they would have conducted a soul-calling ceremony, or *hu plig*, for each of their newborn children. The *hu plig* is conducted three days after birth and could be compared to a baptism in the Christian belief system. Because souls have a tendency to wander off, the Hmong want to guard against the possibility that the soul gets lost or falls into a hole and is unable to return. Hemp strings are tied around the wrists of the child and family members as a protective bond. In some cases, the child is given his or her first silver necklace as a way to bind the soul to the body.

Shoua and Mai now have four children together. His persistence, stemming from simply seeing Mai in a video, certainly paid off. Since his wedding ceremony, Shoua has returned to Laos three times; once to bring 'Ge' to the US, another time to visit his in laws and the third to visit family for information for this book.

Figure 10,   Benjamin holds baby Sarah and sits next to brother
Abraham. Rebeka, the latest addition to the Her household, is not
shown.
Photo courtesy of Shoua Her

Chapter 12
Looking Back, Moving Forward

In many ways, Shoua was very lucky. He didn't starve to death, die of tuberculosis or dysentery or get shot by a border guard. He didn't drown trying to cross the Mekong River, explode in a land mine or any of the other myriad ways of dying so many of his fellow Hmong faced. He didn't die an agonizing death from the toxins being sprayed over villages and jungles, anywhere the Hmong might be hiding. He lost both of his parents and the better part of his childhood, but he survived.

Timing is critical. If the Her clan had been closer to the front of the line during the massacre on the bridge, they may have been mowed down by machine guns. If Shoua had encountered the tiger just a little earlier, perhaps the giant cat would have been frustrated by having his meal interrupted and attacked Shoua to fill its belly. And if the family had been in the jungle a few years after their escape they may have fallen victim to a horrific new tactic of war that decimated so many of his people. The soviet-made chemical agents known as "yellow rain" were sprayed over the fleeing Hmong from aircraft. The toxins killed them either directly by landing on people's skin or breathed in or indirectly, being transmitted by residue collected on leaves or in the rivers. One of Shoua's cousins recalled seeing yellow residue on leaves near the river where he drank and bathed. The poisons caused vomiting, bloody diarrhea, burning sensation of the eyes, coughing and chest pain, fever and dizziness. When exposed to a lethal amount, it could take hours to die. The United States could find no "proof" that these toxins existed and didn't acknowledge the existence of Yellow Rain until many years later.

Another change that occurred after Shoua's move were the circumstances within the camps. In the years following Shoua's safe passage to America, conditions in the refugee camps changed significantly for Hmong who fled after him, in the 1980s and '90s. Jane Hamilton-Merritt sums it up well in her thorough book, *Tragic Mountains*:

> Refugees who had crossed into Thailand in 1975 and 1976 reported few instances of brutality by Thai people. The somewhat friendly Thai attitude toward tribal refugees began to change in 1978. The Thais discovered refugees as a source of money and valuables. They also discovered that refugees had no rights, no recourse to abuses, no ability to bring charges against thieves, murderers, extortionists or rapists.

> After the slaughter at Phou Bia*, those who survived the trek to cross into Thailand often found they were still not safe. Thai villagers and Thai defense forces, armed but not trained, scouted for Hmong crossing into Thailand. Surrounding new arrivals, some *Aw Saw*, local defense forces, made refugees strip naked. Sometimes these men gang-raped the prettiest girls and women. They often took all valuables, particularly silver earrings and necklaces and the ancestral bars of silver, the last store of Hmong family resource. These treasured silver bars, usually owned by families for generations, were often the total inheritance given to a child by his father or mother, to be used only in extreme emergencies (p.476).

*Phou Bia is the site where one Pathet Lao defector estimated that 50,000 Hmong had died from poisoning and another 45,000 had been shot, starved or were tortured to death.

It is staggering to think of the challenges faced by Hmong and other refugees who have somehow made their way to the United States. The stories of hardship and survival, adversity and courage are remarkable. Shoua has done well for himself, coming from one of the poorest countries in the world with an annual per capita income under US $1000. For many years he served as a Victims Assistance Services Project Director at the Asian Pacific Development Center in Denver, Colorado. He and Mai have four children and live in a 3,500 square foot home. He proudly explains that he saved $100,000 by waiting for the drop in the housing market before he purchased his home and took advantage of the first-time home buyers' opportunities. In addition to his full-time job, he and his wife at one point opened a party store. One of the items for sale included a product Shoua developed himself; When their first child, Benjamin, was a baby Shoua would often be out in the garage, working on his older model Jeep Cherokee to squeeze as many miles from it as possible. His wife would call to him to help with the baby. By the time he managed to wash the dirt, grease, and grime from his hands, the crisis had passed. This happened enough times that, to the relief of his wife, Shoua created a hand lotion that he applies before working on his engine or painting the house or any other dirty chore. His product, Liquid Hand Protector (LHP) allows him to wash his hands clean immediately. He speculates that this saved a lot of tension in his family. It is this type of ingenuity, tireless hard work and effort that is reflected in Shoua's story of triumph over adversity.

Shoua has assisted victims of robbery and trespassing, domestic violence survivors and families affected by vehicular homicide, manslaughter and assaults. He has spoken to large groups of newly minted US citizens, sharing his experience and offering motivation and insights he has learned. houa has managed federal grant monies and coordinated efforts with politicians, the FBI, attorneys and US Immigration and Customs Enforcement (ICE). He coordinated cases with international consulates as they arrange for emergency travel visas and unravel complicated passport issues. Local law enforcement in the Denver community has turned to Shoua for guidance. There was the case of a Hmong family reported by neighbors for animal abuse because they killed a chicken in their back yard. Shoua's role was to explain to the police that animal sacrifice is common in shamanism and the family was practicing a healing ritual. Once the police understood it was a cultural issue, they had the information to handle the situation appropriately. Without an understanding of the cultural context, realizing that the shaman was trying to trade the soul of the chicken for the soul of the sick family member, the act would appear frighteningly barbaric to American eyes. Similarly, the parents of school children from some traditional Asian cultures are reported for child abuse because of round bruises on their backs. The marks come from cupping, a healing practice involving suction on the skin designed to treat stagnation of energy and muscle adhesions and relieve tension. Having cultural dialogue and understanding can help alleviate imposing consequences and sanctions that may not be necessary or appropriate.

Other cases of child abuse are legitimate through American eyes and merely good parenting in the eyes of the Hmong. Children are very loved in traditional Hmong culture. Families are large, often with ten or more children, which was helpful in having more hands to help with the fields. Older children were disciplined by their parents- and teachers when the children were in school - with corporal punishment. Beatings were given to encourage the child to behave, to try harder, to learn a lesson. Many Hmong parents expressed confusion when they arrived in the United States. If they weren't allowed to hit their children, how would they learn? Many Hmong parents watched with dismay as their children, seduced by the materialism and individualism of America began to identify with American culture more strongly than Hmong culture. Some lost their children to Hmong gangs as traditional family structure, parenting and values eroded in their new environment.

Refugees who are victims of crime, including women who suffer from domestic violence, are afraid to call the police. In their homeland, police and military were very often the perpetrators of violence and assault, so calling on them in times of vulnerability and protection is a foreign idea. The perpetrator of the violence (usually the husband) will threaten to have the victim deported if she calls for help, a cruel but effective enticement for silence. Language is also a barrier due to the many different languages spoken throughout Asia and transplanted to neighborhoods throughout the US. There is a lack of interpreters who speak Hmong and other Asiatic languages and dialects which affects courts, hospitals, schools, and social service agencies. Despite these and other challenges, people survive, and even thrive. Hmong home ownership, for example, was 43.6% in 2013, up from 13% in 1990. The percentage of Hmong living below the poverty rate, while still significantly larger than the average US population, fell from nearly 70% in 1989 to less than 25% in 2013.

While Shoua's story took place many years ago, the refugee crisis is far from over. Hmong have been forcibly repatriated to Laos from Thailand to face an unwelcoming government. In the early 2000s, reports were still coming in of families who were trying to relocate *within* their home country of Laos but were refused by the locals in the area. The news during the writing of this book is peppered with stories of refugees from Syria trying to cross the Mediterranean into Northern Africa and Europe in rafts and fishing boats. They are in desperate need of sanctuary as they flee for their lives. They also bring with them a myriad of financial, social and medical complications that burden a host country. No one seems to want them.

Shoua is one of the success stories. He and his family live in a typical American house. He drives his jeep to work every day and pays his bills on time. He makes sure his children do their homework and go to bed at a reasonable hour. Yet his in-laws still pull out the tongue of a chicken after it's been killed to examine clues for their future. They peer at the soft bones in its neck or the arrangement of the chicken's feet to determine if their luck will be good or bad. It is hard to break from all the traditions of a people. The Hmong, both Christian and shaman, consulted water buffalo horns in Laos and chicken bones and feet in America to divine their future. In this way, Shoua's family, like so many refugee and immigrant families before him have accepted and become a part of the American dream and lifestyle while keeping hold of many of the values and traditions that make up their identity. Hmong today are defining who they are and what it means to be Hmong. Some agencies, such as the Hmong Cultural Center in St. Paul, Minnesota, teach the Hmong language and traditional arts such as embroidery and *qeej*, the reeded instrument, so that the culture remains alive and vibrant through the generations.

It is a balancing act to learn and accept a new country's language, past times and ideals while retaining the vestiges of home. Maintaining language, religion, food and values can be very challenging for any immigrant group adjusting to a new land.

There are still Hmong who live in Laos. According to our guide, the Lao government helped Hmong resettle in the country in 2003. Some live in cities, working as tour guides to tourists. Others live in traditional villages with over a hundred families or as few as six. While many still live in thatched bamboo huts with pounded earthen floors, pigs and chickens scurrying about, they wear western clothing, use cell phones and are exposed to people from different cultures. Many Hmong who reside in Laos today make a prosperous living by "sending costumes, herbal medicines, and recorded music to relatives living abroad for resale." While Shoua still has cousins living in Laos, his immediate family has immigrated to the United States.

As of this writing, only three of Shoua's siblings have survived. All three sisters live in California; Sue, Chue (whose little girl Bao was given opium to keep her quiet and the family safe), and Phoua, who spent many years in a refugee camp with her husband before they were able to come to the US in the 1990s. Many of the siblings died before Shoua was born or when he was too young to have any memory of them. He remembers the life and death of his older sister, Pa. Although Pa was a Christian, she was obligated to practice shamanism when she was married because that was the belief system of her husband. Her husband's parents were addicted to opium and stole from the entire family in order to support their habit. Pa had married into a violent family, suffering savage beatings from her husband, sometimes while being held down by her in-laws. After her husband took a second wife, Pa fled the abusive marriage, taking their son with her. When she arrived in her home village, her husband came after her and Pa's family forced her to go back with him. Years later, Shoua and his sisters Su and Chue sent money to Pa to buy water buffalo to use for rice farming. When Pa went into the city of Kilometer 52 to pick up the money, she reportedly died after falling from a taxi. Her death seems all the more tragic after such a difficult life.

Vang died of neck cancer and another brother, Chong Houa, drowned in a river near the family village. Chong Houa had struggled crossing that river two times before. The first time was during a fishing expedition in which a grenade was thrown into the water. Chong Houa's job was to swim and collect the fish that floated to the surface after the explosion stunned or killed them. Sometime during the swim he lost his strength and, exhausted from his efforts, had to pull himself onto a rock to rest. He was eventually able to swim back to shore. (Another man, diving for the bigger fish that sank to the bottom after the concuss of the hand grenade, dove twice to retrieve the fish. After his third dive, he never returned.) During the second close call, Chong Houa was in a bamboo raft when it became stuck in the river. Another man jumped in to untangle the craft and release it back to the current. The man had placed a piece of bamboo between his teeth before entering the water in the belief that the Dragon who lives in the water would mistake him for a goat and leave him alone. Since goats and dragons are enemies, it was in the man's interests to be mistaken for a goat. The piece of bamboo must have worked because everyone survived that foray into the water. The third and fatal time occurred when Chong Houa was visiting another village. While there, he learned the Pathet Lao were approaching his family's village and he wanted desperately to warn them. He had two choices; either cross the river the easy way, by boat, or ferry himself across by bamboo raft. He would have preferred to take a boat, but the excursion entailed hiking far downriver to the boat crossing and then boating back upriver, a half day's journey in all. The raft option was dangerous, especially since it was the rainy season and the river was swollen, but it would only take him half an hour or so to reach his family. According to Hmong beliefs, if he had survived that river crossing he would have been safe during future voyages over the water, as the Dragon gives up trying to get people after their third attempt. Chong Houa's raft capsized and his body was found two weeks later, partly buried in silt on the other side of the river. He never made it to issue his dire warning.

There is a cousin who has fished for years in the same area of the river where Chong Houa drowned. A large rock used to stick out of the embankment, a solid part of the landscape since the cousin had first begun fishing that spot. One day not long after Chong Houa's death, the cousin was surprised to see that the rock had cracked and fallen into the river. He believes it was struck by lightning.

Shoua shares a story that highlights the differences in his life, then and now. His oldest son, Benjamin, pushed his plate of chicken nuggets aside. "I'm not hungry", he pouted. Shoua sighed and decided it was time for his son to hear about reality. "When I was your age," Shoua said gently, "we had very little to eat. Many times we had only a cup of rice. Sometimes we had a small bird, no bigger than that." He pointed out the window to a hedge sparrow. "We split it, 4 or 5 of us."

"But it's so little!" Benjamin said, wide eyed.

"Yes. We would mostly eat the rice and then sometimes suck on the little leg bones of the bird to get the flavor of some meat." Shoua gazed off into the distance, remembering. "Eat your chicken nuggets, son."

Other refugees share similar surreal conversations with their children who were born in the United States. The communication and cultural distance that exists between the generations can be in equal parts amusing and heart wrenching. Reem, a refugee from Iraq, shares her experience with her early-teen-age daughter. The mother was instructing her daughter, trying to teach her something. In the mother's traditional culture, a child would never make eye contact with a parent (or a teacher, a boss, any adult in a position of authority) in such a situation as it would be considered very rude and disrespectful. This woman explained, "I realized that as I was trying to instruct her, she was looking right at me! I was furious- how could she be so disrespectful? And then it dawned on me…. She's an American." Because the daughter was raised in the United States, she has learned the culture and customs of this country, not her mother's. It is in moments like these that immigrants and refugees realize they inhabit a very different world from their children.

This kind of break in traditions along generational lines is quite common in families who immigrate, whether as refugees or not. Interestingly, if a child is born in a foreign land and moves to the US (or elsewhere) when very young, they are considered a 1.5 generation. While they are not truly a first generation, since they were not born in the new country, they were raised in it and for all intents and purposes are assimilated into the host country, thus the "1.5". The rapid assimilation of youth into the host country is both a source of pride and anxiety for parents and grandparents. They are pleased their youth are adapting to a new way of life, learning English, becoming educated and hopefully having the better life every parent dreams for their children. But this comes at a cost. The young generation raised in America often loses the language of their people. The children sometimes become interpreters for their parents or grandparents who may not speak English. While convenient for schools and courts where an interpreter may not be readily available, this practice is problematic. The obvious issue is the validity of what the child translates. Did the teacher really say the child is doing well in school? But more disturbingly, it changes the traditional power balance in the family. Now it is the child who is placed in the position of authority, a far cry from the role in their homeland.

Additionally, traditional ceremonies and foods may seem quaint, or worse- an embarrassment. The "Americanized" children are more materialistic than their parents or grand-parents, yearn for independence and an individualistic identity rather than a collective one. In other words, most traditional Asian cultures value what's good for the group –in this case, the family- outweighs the good of the individual. If a child is needed to come home after school to care for a younger sibling that is more important than their desire to go out and play with friends. Children and teens who have been indoctrinated to American tradition resist being "deprived of their freedom", time with friends and carefree childhood. So, while immigrant and refugee families often find more opportunity for education, economic growth and cultural or religious expression, it comes at a cost. These issues are common to many relative newcomers, not just the Hmong community.

Depression and Post Traumatic Stress Disorder (PTSD) are common issues among many refugees, including the Hmong. Survivor guilt, troubled sleep, physical manifesta-tion of internal stress (called somatization) such as headaches or body aches are common experiences. The mind and body are seen as connected in eastern culture much more so than in the west where we visit a medical doctor for physical problems and a psychiatrist or therapist to deal with emo-tional issues. Refugees from some countries struggle with depression as a result of seeing extreme violence, often right in front of them. Yet they come from cultures where being diagnosed with depression is synonymous with being crazy.

It is very challenging to seek and receive the help needed from a professional if it is considered shameful to do so.

I have had the honor of hearing Shoua as he shares his story every semester with the students of my Multicultural Issues classes. At the end of one of his talks, one of the students raised her hand and asked Shoua how he has dealt with the many traumas he has faced. Shoua responded by asking for two pages of blank notebook paper. After she handed them to him, Shoua crumpled one up into a tight ball and then opened it again. He encouraged the students

Figure 1, Picture of Shoua Her in front of paj ntaub displayed at the Asian Pacific Development Center in Aurora, Colorado
Photo taken by the author, permission of the Asian Pacific Development Center, Aurora, Colorado

to see how wrinkled and unusable it now was. Then he held up the fresh sheet of lined paper with no wrinkles, ready for note taking. He simply stated, with a smile on his face, that when you are faced with the crumpled sheet of paper you pick up a fresh sheet. You start over. The students clapped.

Acknowledgments

I would like to thank my husband Steve for his enthusiasm during our research trip to Laos, to my daughter Anna Marie, Mom (Sue) and John Pankonin and longtime friend Andy Hill for support and for providing feedback at several important junctures in the writing process. I'm grateful to Metropolitan State University of Denver for approving the sabbatical leave that made this journey–and this book–possible.

Many individuals and organizations contributed to the research and information provided in this book. Special thanks go to Dr. Robert Cooper, whose details, photos and generosity are greatly appreciated. Appreciation goes to Mr. Kham Dee of Tiger Trail (tour agency), a Hmong guide who led us to several native villages in Laos. Thanks to Mark Pfeifer and Txong Pao Lee of the Hmong Cultural Center of Minnesota in St. Paul where I was given a "Hmong 101" training, and allowed open access to their extensive library on Hmong culture. The "We Are Hmong" exhibit at the Minnesota History Center, Traditional Arts and Ethnology Centre in Luang Prabang, Laos, Lao National Museum and the COPE Visitor Centre (Cooperative Orthotic & Prosthetic Enterprise) in Vientiane, Laos, all provided insight into the culture and history of the Hmong.

Interviews are my favorite way of obtaining information, as firsthand accounts offer such interesting detail. I am grateful to Paul Stein who provided information on interviewing asylum seekers and the process of determining who the legitimate candidates are. Dee Daniels Scriven explained the services after the 1980 Refugee Act was passed. Andy Irwin was instrumental in connecting me with Don Nelson, the pilot who shared his story of the L 19 Birddog plane in Vietnam with the Forward Air Control. Reem Mahmood shared cultural differences she experienced after she entered the US as a refugee from Iraq. Ms. Mahmood now works as a Program Specialist helping TANFF recipients. Refugees connected with the African Cultural Center in Colorado graciously shared their stories in a public panel presentation on MSU Denver's campus in the spring of 2015. Caren Lindfors, RN, provided me with information about Hmong childbirth and labor and Christine Moua graciously shared her family's story of escape.

My biggest debt of gratitude goes to Shoua Her, who answered my endless questions, recalled painful memories and recounted traumatic events on a great number of occasions. He did all of this with great grace and patience. I am grateful to the larger Hmong community–for their story, their fortitude and their survival.

References

Alford, J. & Duguid, N. (2000). Hot Sour Salty Sweet; A Culinary Journey Through Southeast Asia. Workman Publishing, Inc., NY., NY.

Baird, I.G. *The Hmong Come to Southern Laos; Local Responses and the Creation of Racialized Boundaries*, Hmong Studies Journal, Volume 11:1-38, University of Wisconsin-Madison

Bloom, G., Bush, A., Stewart, I., & Waters, R. (2015) Vietnam, Cambodia, Laos & Northern Thailand, Lonely Planet Publications, China.

Cha, D. & Livo, N.J. (2000) Teaching with Folk Stories of the Hmong (Activity Book), Libraries Unlimited, Inc., Englewood, Colorado

Cooper, R. (2008). The Hmong; a guide to traditional life. Lao Insight Books, Lao People's Democratic Republic.

Davis, C. O., (1996) Across the Mekong; The True Story of an Air America Helicopter Pilot, Hildesigns Press, Charlottesville, Virginia

Denver Museum of Nature and Science, *Mythic Creatures* Exhibit

Denver Museum of Nature and Science, *The Power of Poison* Exhibit

Faderman, L. (1998). I Begin My Life All Over; The Hmong and the American Immigrant Experience; Beacon Press, Boston, Mass

Fadiman, A. (1997)The Spirit Catches You and You Fall Down; A Hmong Child, Her American Doctors, and the Collision of Two Cultures, Farrar, Straus and Giroux, New York

Gladwell, M. (2008) Outliers; The Story of Success, Little, Brown and Company, New York

Hamilton-Merritt, J. (1993). Tragic Mountains; The Hmong, the Americans, and the Secret Wars for Laos, 1942-1992; Indiana University Press

Her, V. K., & Buley-Meissner, M.L., Eds. (2012), Hmong and American; from Refugees to Citizens, The Minnesota Historical Society Press, Minnesota

Hmong Cultural Center: St. Paul, Minnesota

Kim, B.S.K., Atkinson, D.R., & Umemoto, D. (2001). *Asian Cultural Values and counseling process: Current knowledge and directions for future research.* The Counseling Psychologist, Volume 29, 570-603.

Kim, B.S.K., Ng, G.F., & Ahn, A.J., (Spring, 2009). *Client adherence to Asian Cultural Values, Common Factors in Counseling, and Session Outcome With Asian American Clients at a University Counseling Center.* Journal of Counseling & Development, Volume. 87, Number 2, 131-142.

Lao National Unexploded Ordinance Programme (UXO Lao) Annual Report, Vientiane, Laos

Livo, N.J., & Cha, D. (1991). Folk Stories of the Hmong, Libraries Unlimited, Inc., Englewood, Colorado

Kos. T. (2013). Hmong Wedding Procedures; Hmong Cultural Center, St. Paul, Minn.

Kurlansky, M. (2002). Salt; A World History; Penguin Books, NY, NY

Lao National Museum, Vientiane, Laos

Minnesota History Center; *We Are Hmong* exhibit June, 2015

Pehu, E. *Upland Agriculture Lao PDR* Regional Environmental Technical Assistance 5771 Poverty Reduction & Environmental Management in Remote Greater Mekong Subregion (GMS) Watersheds Project (Phase I)   file:///C:/Users/Lbutler6/ Downloads/0002998-farming-upland-agriculture-lao-pdr.pdf

Personal Interviews, Shoua Her, Txongpao Lee & Mark Pfeifer (Hmong Cultural Center, St. Paul, Minn.), Paul Stein (Immigration Officer), Caren Lindfors, RN

Phan, L. T., Rivera, E. T., Roberts-Wilbur, J. (Summer, 2005). *Understanding Vietnamese Refugee Women's Identity Development From a Sociopolitical and Historical Perspective,* Journal of Counseling & Development, Volume 83, Number 3, 305-312.

Po Cha, Y., An Introduction to Hmong Culture (2010). McFarland & Company, Inc., Publishers, Jefferson, North Carolina

Publicly shared stories by refugees

Quincy, K. Harvesting Pa Chay's Wheat; The Hmong and America's Secret War in Laos (2000), Eastern Washington University Press, Spokane, Washington

Quincy, K. Hmong; History of a People (1995). Eastern Washington University Press, Spokane, Washington

Rollins, J. (Feb. 2009). *A Reality Too Horrible to Consider*, Counseling Today

Seuling, B. (1978). The Last Cow on the White House Lawn & Other Little Known Facts About the Presidency. Double Day and Company, NY, NY.

Shah, A. *The Thread that Binds* (Dec. 5, 2012), The Star Tribune

Smith, J. E. (2013), Eisenhower in War and Peace, Random House, New York

South-East Asia on a Shoestring (1999), Lonely Planet Publications, Oakland, CA

Spoerri, P. (2009). *The Geneva Conventions of 1949: origins and current significance* International Committee of the Red Cross https://www.icrc.org/eng/resources/documents/statement/geneva-conventions-statement-120809.htm

Stories of the Mekong (2009) Cultural Heritage for Sustainable Development, a program of Museum Cooperation in Southeast Asia (MuSEA), Vietnam

Sue, D. & Sue, D. (2013), Counseling the Culturally Diverse (6th Ed.), John Wiley & Sons, Hoboken, NJ.

The Diplomat (article on landmines) http://thediplomat.com/2013/04/landmines-still-blight-southeast-asia/

Video, Carved in Silence (1987)

Warner, R. (1996), Shooting at the Moon; The Story of America's Clandestine War in Laos. Steerforth Press, Vermont

Willcox, D. (1986). Hmong Folklife; Hmong Natural Association of North Carolina

Yang, K. (2008). The Latehomecomer; A Hmong Family Memoir. Coffee House Press, Minneapolis, MN

Refugee Camps are a Breeding Ground for Disease (2015) retrieved from http://learningenglish.voanews.com/content/refugee-camps-are-a-breeding-ground-for-disease/1514910.html

Map of bombed areas in Laos from: http://legaciesofwar.org/about-laos/secret-war-laos/

http://www.guaduabamboo.com/uses/products-made-from-bamboo

http://planesoffame.org/index.php?mact=staircraft,cntnt01,default,0&cntnt01what=stplanes&cntnt01alias=O-1E-L-19&cntnt01returnid=128   (About the Birddog planes)

ABOUT THE AUTHOR

Dr. Lynann H. Butler is a tenured professor, mental health and addictions counselor, international speaker, and the President of Professional Counseling Services. She enjoys sharing her wisdom, mistakes, and humor with students and mentees. She lives with her family and assortment of rescue pets in Denver, Colorado.

JOURNEY INSTITUTE PRESS

Journey Institute Press is a non-profit publishing house created by authors to flip the publishing model for new authors. Created with intention and purpose to provide the highest quality publishing resources available to authors whose stories might otherwise not be told.

JI Press focusses on women, BIPOC, and LGBTQ+ authors without regard to the genre of their work.

As a Publishing House, our goal is to create a supportive, nurturing, and encouraging environment that puts the author above the publisher in the publishing model.

Storytellers Publishing is an Imprint of Journey Institute Press, a division of 50 in 52 Journey, Inc.

NOTE: The world of publishing has changed dramatically. This has also affected authors and their ability to let readers know about their books. Today, most people buy books based on word of mouth. If you would like to help this author, please consider leaving an honest review of this book on retail sites and book community sites.

www.ingramcontent.com/pod-product-compliance
Lightning Source LLC
Chambersburg PA
CBHW051625120626
46551CB00014B/1937